ESSENTIAL HISTORIES

The Soviet–Afghan War 1979–89

Gregory Fremont-Barnes

OSPREY PUBLISHING
Bloomsbury Publishing Plc
Kemp House, Chawley Park, Cumnor Hill, Oxford OX2 9PH, UK
29 Earlsfort Terrace, Dublin 2, Ireland
1385 Broadway, 5th Floor, New York, NY 10018, USA
E-mail: info@ospreypublishing.com
www.ospreypublishing.com

OSPREY is a trademark of Osprey Publishing Ltd

First published in Great Britain in 2024

© Osprey Publishing Ltd, 2024

The text in this edition is revised and updated from: ESS 75: *The Soviet–Afghan War 1979–89* (Osprey Publishing, 2012).

Essential Histories Series Editor: Professor Robert O'Neill

A catalogue record for this book is available from the British Library.

ISBN: PB 9781472861801;
eBook 9781472861818;
ePDF 9781472861849;
XML 9781472861825;
Audio 9781472861832

24 25 26 27 28   10 9 8 7 6 5 4 3 2 1

Cover design by Stewart Larking
Maps by Peter Bull Art Studio, revised by www.bounford.com
Index by Alison Worthington
Typeset by PDQ Digital Media Solutions, Bungay, UK
Printed and bound in India by Replika Press Private Ltd.

To find out more about our authors and books visit www.ospreypublishing.com. Here you will find extracts, author interviews, details of forthcoming events and the option to sign up for our newsletter.

CONTENTS

INTRODUCTION

Its significance often overlooked, the Soviet–Afghan War stands as one of the seminal events of the last quarter of the 20th century. In less than a decade it exposed fatal defects in the Soviet political structure as well as in communist ideology itself, helped trigger and sustain the policy of internal reform led by Mikhail Gorbachev (1931–2022) from 1985, contributed strongly to the collapse of the Communist Party and the consequent end to the Cold War and, finally, played a decisive contributing role in the disintegration of the USSR. The conflict rapidly involved other nations with strong political interests at stake in Central Asia, not least the United States, which clandestinely siphoned billions of dollars in aid to the Mujahideen through Pakistan. Pakistan itself not only strongly supported the resistance in general, but particularly those elements of religious extremists who in the wake of Soviet withdrawal took a prominent part in the internecine struggle between rival Mujahideen factions which ultimately led to the Taliban's triumph in the autumn of 1996. In short, the network that became al-Qaeda took root as a direct consequence of the Soviet–Afghan War, in which Osama bin Laden and others like him provided substantial funds to large numbers of *jihadi*.

The international implications soon became apparent. Quite apart from the horrific wave of repression which their regime unleashed, the Taliban offered Afghanistan as a training and recruiting ground for other extremist groups whose political and ideological agenda stretched far beyond the borders of their war-ravaged country. By hosting al-Qaeda on Afghan soil, the Taliban sowed the seeds for the terrorist attacks of 11 September 2001, which in turn triggered a devastating reaction from the United States and the United Kingdom, soon followed

OPPOSITE
Tough, resourceful, and inured to hard living, the Mujahideen possessed many qualities which compensated for sophisticated Soviet weaponry and more reliable logistic and communication systems. (Photo by Pascal Manoukian/ Sygma via Getty Images)

Recognizing the folly of the war as ideologically unsound and economically unsustainable, Mikhail Gorbachev drew the correct conclusion and withdrew Soviet forces from Afghanistan. (Photo by Peter Turnley/Corbis/VCG via Getty Images)

by other NATO powers. All of this 'Pandora's box' may be traced to the Soviet invasion of Afghanistan and the ghastly war it inaugurated.

The foundations of a full understanding of the West's involvement in Afghanistan in the early 21st century must rest upon a firm grasp of the causes, course, and outcome of the Soviet–Afghan War. The lessons from this confirmed the folly that underpinned Soviet strategy: unrealistic political aims, pursued by armed forces unable to cope with the unconventional methods of an adversary which, though vastly disadvantaged in weapons and technology, managed to overcome the odds through sheer tenacity and an unswerving devotion to freedom and faith.

In 1979, political leaders in Moscow directed a sceptical military to intervene in the Afghan civil war in order to maintain in power a nominally communist regime in Kabul, which was struggling against a resistance movement of disparate groups known collectively as the Mujahideen or 'fighters for the faith'. Deeply unpopular with large swathes of rural, deeply conservative, tribal peoples stretched across a country divided on religious, ethnic and tribal lines, Nur Mohammad Taraki's (1917–79) government of the Democratic Republic of Afghanistan (DRA) controlled urban areas but very little of the countryside, where tribal elders and clan chiefs held sway. Even within the Communist Party apparatus, rival factions grappled for sole control of the affairs of state, denying them the time or ability to implement the socialist reforms they espoused, including the emancipation of women, land redistribution, and the dismantling of traditional societal structures in favour of a more egalitarian alternative. None of these reforms resonated with a traditional, Islamic nation, whose opposition manifested its outrage in open civil war. Taraki was overthrown by his own prime minister – a member of the opposing communist faction – but he proved even less effective at imposing rule than his predecessor. Lack of political direction and anger at unwanted reforms precipitated mutinies and mass desertions within the army and outbreaks of bloody revolt in cities, towns, and villages across the country, which the Soviets immediately appreciated as a threat to their influence over a neighbouring state sharing a border with three of the USSR's Muslim republics.

Leonid Brezhnev (1906–82), the General Secretary of the Communist Party of the Soviet Union, concerned at the disintegrating situation in Afghanistan and determined to maintain a sphere of influence over the region, ordered an invasion – despite the fact that neither the climate nor the terrain suited Soviet equipment or tactics. When Soviet troops rolled over the border in December 1979, ostensibly in aid of a surrogate government in Kabul, they expected to conduct a brief, largely bloodless campaign with highly sophisticated mechanized and air assault forces, easily capable of crushing Afghan resistance in a matter of months before enabling a newly installed government to tackle the resistance thereafter. Events exploded at least two myths prevalent in the West: the Soviets never intended to remain long in Afghanistan, as supposed in Washington, and their relatively small troop numbers attested to this fact. Nor did the invasion represent the belated realization of the historic Russian drive to establish a warm-water port on the Indian Ocean. Theirs was to be a temporary – albeit an internationally condemned – presence.

Yet the Soviets comprehensively failed to appreciate the quagmire in which they found themselves. Their forces possessed very limited combat experience – none at all in counterinsurgency – and they foolishly assumed their successful interventions in East Germany in 1954, in Hungary in 1956, and in Czechoslovakia in 1968 offered models for any military operation executed against a popular struggle. Western analysts, too, predicted Soviet victory, but the political and military circumstances behind the Iron Curtain offered no parallels with Afghanistan. Unlike the Soviets' client states in Eastern Europe, Afghanistan stood embroiled in the midst of a civil war – not a straightforward, effectively unarmed, insurrection – and thus applying simple but

Soviet tanks in Kabul. Afghan terrain proved almost entirely unsuited to armour, which could defend roads and main areas of concentration, but encountered serious difficulty manoeuvring in mountainous terrain. (Bettmann/Getty Images)

overwhelming military might could only guarantee protection for the central government in Kabul, and perhaps control of larger cities and towns, but not the countryside. Soviet intervention in December 1979 achieved its initial objective with predictable ease: elite troops overthrew the government, seized the presidential palace and key communications centres, killed the head of state, Hafizullah Amin (1929–79), and replaced him with a Soviet-sponsored successor.

The plan thereafter seemed straightforward: stabilize the political situation, strengthen, retrain and enlarge DRA forces to enable them to quell the insurgency on their own while concurrently performing the more passive roles of garrison duty and, finally, protect the country's key infrastructure such as major roads, dams and its sources of electricity and gas. Thus, within three years, the Soviets, confident in the notion that the Afghan government could stand on its own feet when backed by the continued presence of Soviet advisors including army officers, KGB personnel, and civilian specialists in engineering, medicine, education and other spheres, and furnished with a continuous supply of arms and technology, believed their forces could withdraw across the border, leaving a friendly, stable, compliant and ideologically like-minded regime firmly in power behind them.

None of these objectives stood up to the reality of the situation, however. The civil war continued to spiral beyond the government's ability to suppress it and the DRA forces' morale plummeted further, decreasing their operational effectiveness and causing concern in Moscow that withdrawing its troops would amount to both humiliation and the collapse of all Soviet influence over its client state. Thus, what began as a fairly simple military operation – overthrowing a government and occupying key positions throughout the country, a task which the Soviet military, trained in large-scale, high-tempo operations, could manage with ease – soon developed into a protracted, costly and ultimately unwinnable fiasco. The conflict pitted small, ill-armed but highly motivated guerrilla forces – employing fighting methods bearing no relation to those practised by opponents trained and armed to fight in central Europe – against troops of utterly different organization and doctrine. Experience soon demonstrated the limited efficacy of heavy infantry, tanks, artillery, and jet fighters in a struggle that decisively depended upon more helicopter gunships, more heliborne troops, and more special forces to meet the demands of the fluid, asymmetric war conducted by the Mujahideen.

As the years passed and casualties steadily mounted, the war graphically exposed the weaknesses of the Soviets' strategy and the poorly suited structure of their armed forces, which never succeeded in overcoming an ever-growing resistance movement operating over a vast, varied, and exceedingly challenging landscape. Indeed, both Soviet tactics and strategy contained fatal flaws. Their doctrine directed the use of armoured and motor-rifle (i.e motorized) units to advance along narrow axes, maintaining secure lines of communication while wreaking destruction upon any resistance they encountered through combined arms (the co-ordination of firepower offered by infantry, artillery, armour, and air assault units). With little experience or training in a counterinsurgency role, the Soviet armed forces chose a simplistic approach to the problem: they merely cleared territory in their path, which translated into the widespread killing of civilians, as well as resistance fighters – who avoided where possible the superior weight of fire which their opponents could bring to bear. Everywhere circumstances appeared to confirm Alexander the Great's dictum that 'one can occupy Afghanistan, but one cannot vanquish her'.

Civilians who survived the onslaught naturally fled, embittered, abandoning their destroyed villages and property to seek refuge in cities or over the border. Such ruthless exploitation of air and artillery power was deliberately meant to clear areas, particularly along the border with Pakistan, so as to deprive the resistance of recruits and local support as well as to aid in the interdiction of supplies crossing over into Afghanistan. This strategy caused horrendous human suffering: only six months after the Soviet invasion, approximately 800,000 Afghans had fled into Pakistan.

At the outset of the war the Soviets' strategy involved persuading the population to support the communist-led Kabul government, thus denying aid to the resistance in the anonymity of the provinces. This soon proved unrealistic, not least owing to the regime's heavy-handed measures. They then turned to denying the insurgents supplies, which led to driving civilians off their land or destroying their livelihoods as a warning to withhold their support from the insurgency. This policy also involved interdicting supply routes that connected the insurgents to the vital materiel moving through Pakistan, the principal source of aid to the Mujahideen. The Soviet 40th Army mounted numerous substantial operations against areas known to be actively supporting the

Afghan civilians flee during fighting between rival Mujahideen fighters, including the emergent Taliban, who after the fall of Najibullah's government in 1992 began to vie for national control. (SAEED KHAN/AFP via Getty Images)

resistance and severed supply lines whenever possible, but the 'drip, drip' effect caused by the guerrillas' constant ambushes, sniping, raids, and mine-laying ultimately inflicted unsustainable losses on the invader.

The Soviet–Afghan War differed from other conflicts of the Cold War era. Although it was a limited conflict, it was longer than most – slightly over nine years in length – and thus did not share the decisive nature of the Arab–Israeli wars of 1948, 1956, 1967, and 1973, or the Falklands War of 1982. The Soviet *imbroglio* lacked the scale of the Korean War (1950–53) and did not conclude with a clear political outcome, in contrast to that proxy conflict. Nor can it be seen as some sort of Soviet 'Vietnam', especially in terms of scale. The Soviets never deployed anything approaching the numbers the Americans sent to Southeast Asia between 1965 and 1973, with over half a million personnel by 1968, compared with the average of approximately 118,000 Soviets serving at any given time in Afghanistan. Whereas the Americans conducted numerous operations involving several divisions, the Soviets' entire 40th Army in Afghanistan consisted of a mere five divisions, four independent brigades, and four independent regiments, plus various small support units. Numbers as insufficient as these denied the Soviets – by their own faulty strategic calculations – any realistic chance of securing over 20 provincial centres plus various key industrial sites, to say nothing of the manpower required to secure whole swathes of remote and practically inaccessible territory inhabited by a seething population supporting elusive, seldom-visible opponents who moved by stealth, struck at will, and melted back into civilian life with little or no trace. The protection demanded for hundreds of miles of roads, communication lines, and points of strategic importance – some of which the Soviets had to occupy outright or, at the very least, deny to the Mujahideen – placed a colossal burden on the invaders, who failed to appreciate both the sheer scale of the enterprise and the immense commitment in manpower it required.

BACKGROUND TO WAR
The genesis of Afghan–Russian relations

The roots of Russian intervention in Afghanistan extend back to imperial times, when Tsarist Russia first cast its eyes on Central Asia in the 1730s. Russia undertook the gradual conquest of the region as part of an expansionist programme, which witnessed Russian growth into the Crimea, the Caucasus, and Siberia all the way to the Pacific. By the late 1830s, Russian interest in Afghanistan in particular began to manifest itself. Following the Russo-Persian War of 1826–28, the Russians began to exercise modest influence within government circles in Tehran, and when in 1837 Persian forces sought to capture Herat, in western Afghanistan, Russian advisors and mercenaries accompanied the expedition. Authorities in Calcutta – the capital of British India and the seat of the East India Company, which managed Britain's Indian dominions – concerned at the growing Russian menace to Afghan independence, threatened intervention and managed to instigate a Persian withdrawal, but from this point Anglo-Russian relations began to sour. Herein lay the beginnings of the 'Great Game' – a contest for influence in Central Asia, but specifically over Afghanistan and the unclear border regions on the northern fringes of the Raj. As Russian power expanded inexorably into the Caucasus, Georgia, and Khirgiz, and towards the khanates of Samarkand, Khiva, and Bukhara, the British foresaw the

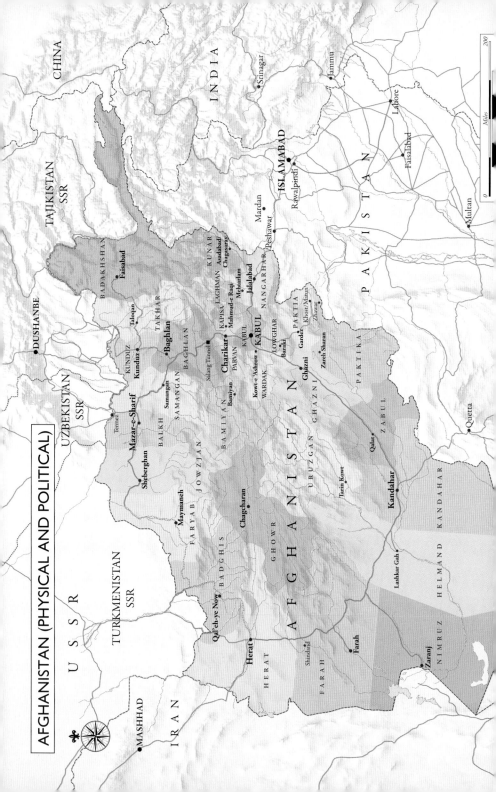

point when their position in India would lie exposed to Russia – once the buffer of Afghanistan fell under the Romanovs' sway. Nor was it inconceivable that the Russians ultimately sought access to a warm-water port by occupying Afghanistan before penetrating south, across what now constitutes Pakistan, to the coast of the Indian Ocean.

British suspicions of Russian intentions took a dramatic turn when British and East India Company forces invaded Afghanistan in 1839 in order to counter perceived Russian influence at the Afghan court. In fact, the Afghans had declined to receive the Russian diplomatic representative at Kabul even before the Anglo-Indian army crossed the frontier, rendering the entire exercise costly and pointless, and bruising Britain's martial reputation after a three-year occupation of Afghanistan. Nevertheless, suspicions of Russian intentions continued thereafter, despite the drubbing inflicted on the tsar by the British and French during the Crimean War (1854–56), which thwarted imperial expansion against Turkey and into the Mediterranean. The war checked Russia's expansion into the Danubian provinces (modern Romania and Bulgaria) and towards the Bosphorus and Dardanelles (the Black Sea Straits), but merely re-directed its energies against Central Asia, so that by 1869 the Russian frontier reached the Amu Darya River (the classical Oxus) on the northern border of Afghanistan, to much alarm in London and Calcutta. The next crisis occurred in 1878, when, in the midst of another war with Turkey in which Russia sought to control the Black Sea Straits, St Petersburg again dispatched a diplomatic mission to Kabul, provoking a second British invasion of Afghanistan. After achieving a rather better military and political outcome than their previous campaign almost 40 years before, the British withdrew in 1881, content with having extracted various concessions, including the right to regulate Afghan foreign policy thereafter. The 'Great Game' cannot be said to have come to an end until 1907 when, with the Anglo-Russian treaty of that year – fresh on the heels of the Russians' decisive defeat at the hands of the Japanese in Manchuria in 1904–05 – St Petersburg declared that Afghanistan stood outside its sphere of influence and promised to consult Britain on all business concerning Russia and Afghanistan. In a *quid pro quo*, Britain pledged neither to occupy nor to annex any Afghan territory nor to meddle in its domestic affairs. Afghanistan did not recognize this agreement, but the terms remained in force between the imperial powers until 1919, when Afghan troops crossed into India and tried to foment an insurrection along the frontier – a matter settled in the very brief Third Anglo-Afghan War (May–August 1919) in which Britain ejected the invaders before agreeing to forswear all control over Afghan foreign policy and thus signifying the country's status as a genuinely sovereign state.

A border crossing at the Khyber Pass, 1919. Such posts only controlled principal road access, just as they would decades later when the Soviets occupied Afghanistan. (Photo by Hulton Archive/ Getty Images)

The war offered the Afghans the opportunity to request military aid from the new Bolshevik government and, while the conflict ended before anything materialized, the episode inaugurated a close relationship between Afghanistan and the Soviet Union. This resulted in

the 1921 Afghan–Soviet Treaty, the first international agreement concluded by the new Soviet state, marking the beginning of economic and military aid to Kabul. Thereafter, the Soviets intervened on two occasions: once in 1925 to occupy a small, disputed island in the Amu Darya, and four years later, after the overthrow of King Amanullah (1892–1960; reigned 1919–29), when a Soviet force intervened in a failed attempt to return him to power. International calls for the troops' withdrawal forced the issue, but in 1930 Soviet troops again crossed the frontier in pursuit of a dissident who sought protection in neutral Afghanistan.

During the 1920s and '30s, the Soviets concentrated on suppressing (successfully) various guerrilla movements that sprang up after the Central Asian territories refused to accept control from Moscow. With British withdrawal from India in 1947 (which led to partition, with Pakistan emerging as Afghanistan's eastern and southern neighbour), the Soviets no longer faced any serious competitor in the region for influence over Afghanistan, and their interest in the area redoubled, particularly after Stalin's death in 1953, when Soviet arms poured into the country as part of a larger financial-aid package and a drive towards increased levels of trade. In January 1954, for example, Prime Minister Daoud secured a Soviet loan of $3.5 million to aid in the construction of two silos and bakeries, while the following year the two countries renewed a barter protocol on commodity exchange that guaranteed Soviet imports, including petroleum, construction materials (especially cement), and metals, in exchange for Afghan wool, raw cotton, and animal hides. In December 1955, the Soviet Union granted a $100 million, long-term development loan for the purpose of undertaking projects jointly agreed by surveyors from both countries. This massive influx of Soviet investment funded the building of roads, river ports, an improved telecommunications network, hydroelectric plants, irrigation dams with canal systems, bridges, hospitals, hydroelectric dams, airfields, and the Salang Pass highway tunnel, which provided a

OVERLEAF
The Salang Pass and Tunnel, the latter of which offered a 1.6-mile route through the mountainous Hindu Kush, thereby connecting the Soviet Union with Kabul. (Jonathan Wilson/ Getty Images)

route through the practically impenetrable Hindu
Kush mountain range from the north. Simultaneously,
Daoud secured a ten-year extension of the 1931 Soviet–

Afghan Treaty of Neutrality and Non-Aggression. In
March 1956, on the strength of recommendations
made by Soviet advisors, the Afghans launched the first

Five Year Plan, a direct parallel to that initiated under Stalin in the 1930s.

Officially, Afghanistan remained a neutral, non-aligned nation, staying aloof from Cold War politics, but in reality it was moving inexorably into the Soviet sphere, not through ideological inclination, but by dint of growing economic dependence. Naturally, the further Soviet–Afghan relations deepened, the stronger Moscow's inclination was to protect its investment by carefully cultivating its neighbour. As with so many other developing nations, the Soviets exploited Afghanistan as a testing ground for the peaceful economic penetration of a 'Third World' nation as part of their worldwide programme of competition with capitalist states. By the early 1960s, many Eastern Bloc products found markets in Afghanistan, especially goods from Czechoslovakia and Poland, both of which provided loans and barter agreements.

As the Americans refused Kabul military assistance, the Afghans naturally turned to the Soviets, who in August 1956 concluded an agreement to supply $25 million in arms, including tanks, bombers, helicopters, and small arms, as well as to provide expertise in constructing or expanding military airfields. The Afghans' dependence on spare parts and technical assistance in turn drew in Soviet military advisors, who served in large numbers attached to Afghan military units and their training establishments, while 4,000 Afghan officers received education and training in the Soviet Union, prompting many, indoctrinated with Marxist principles, to establish a communist party at home on 1 January 1965. By the 1970s, the Soviets had established a strong influence over Afghan affairs, a circumstance that enabled a small group of communist-inspired Afghan army officers to seize control of the government and establish the Democratic Republic of Afghanistan (DRA) in 1978 under Taraki.

The Soviets harboured a strong desire not to forfeit the colossal financial investment made in Afghanistan over more than two decades, and sought to bolster the tenuously established communist regime on its border, which justified their support on ideological grounds. Above all, Moscow hoped to prevent an Islamic government – whether as radical as that ensconced in Tehran in February 1979 or not – from overthrowing Taraki's government. Any such successor government, motivated by militant Islam, would pose a threat to the stability of the Soviet Union's Central Asian republics of Tajikistan, Turkmenistan, and Uzbekistan, which between them accounted for 60 million Muslims spread right across the vulnerable southern flank of the Soviet empire.

Nur Mohammad Taraki. Seizing power in April 1978, his government rapidly alienated large parts of the conservative population over land reform, religion, and women's rights. (Photo by François LOCHON/Gamma-Rapho via Getty Images)

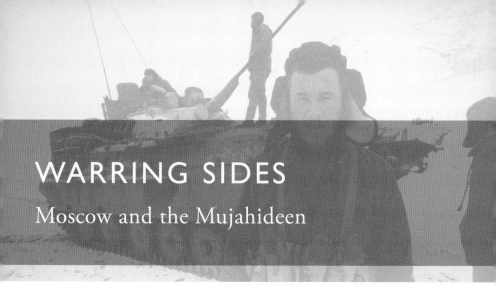

WARRING SIDES
Moscow and the Mujahideen

Soviet forces and their DRA allies

The 40th Army, which represented the Soviets' military presence in Afghanistan, varied in strength, but averaged around 118,000 men in Afghanistan at any given time. These troops were never intended to play the leading role in subduing the Afghan insurgency – that was to remain the primary responsibility of DRA forces – and never anticipated the scale of the enterprise triggered by their appearance on Afghan soil. As a consequence, and because of the Kremlin's steadfast adherence to the original notion that the 40th Army remain a 'limited contingent', these troops failed to establish the substantial presence in the country that subsequent events rendered so necessary. Moreover, with their armed forces structured, equipped, and trained to operate on the northern European plain (or Central Front, in NATO parlance), or alternatively on the plains of northern China as the most likely battlegrounds of the future, Soviet strategists expected to conduct fast-paced conventional operations. They certainly did not anticipate undertaking a low-intensity, asymmetric war in Central Asia, and thus their force structure, weaponry, and tactics necessarily underwent substantial alteration, a programme which of course took time to evolve and implement.

Broadly speaking, Soviet troops engaged in four types of military action in Afghanistan. The first consisted of major operations conducted by both regular and special forces, including artillery and aircraft, and generally in conjunction with DRA units, the purpose being to destroy large groups of Mujahideen in particular areas of the country. Soviet commanders conducted these operations in phases lasting for several weeks or longer. The second type of operation was carried out on a smaller scale, perhaps by a single regiment with artillery and aircraft in support. This type of operation focused on destroying a specific group of rebels in a location discovered via intelligence gathering. Such operations tended to be conducted in ten days or less. Thirdly, while such combat missions were under way, units 'combed' villages in search of concealed weapons caches or medical aid stations. Fourthly, small units, often company-sized, conducted ambushes along roads, on mountain trails, and near villages, with locations selected on the basis of intelligence gathered by Afghan intelligence personnel.

Even so, to a considerable extent the Soviets remained shackled to the methods they knew and understood

Soviet troops often suffered from a lack of training, harsh discipline by draconian officers, and poor medical services, problems sometimes compounded by drug abuse and alcoholism. (Photo by Getty Images)

– large-scale operations in the form of conventional offensives. They continued to launch these regularly, most notably in the Panjshir Valley, despite generally poor results, since none of these major operations achieved more than temporarily neutralizing resistance activity in the areas over which the Soviets' ponderous military machine functioned. Experience revealed that heliborne forces operating in conjunction with mechanized forces could function effectively at the battalion and brigade level, but such methods tended to stifle tactical success when carried out on a divisional or larger scale. Counterinsurgency depends on highly mobile, well-led, well-trained, and suitably equipped forces capable of fighting guerrillas by employing their own methods. Soviet armour, airpower, and heavily laden infantry dependent on their armoured personnel carriers (APCs) for transport over difficult terrain could not, despite their impressive firepower, compensate for their inherent shortcomings in a counterinsurgency environment, for the Mujahideen seldom appeared in concentration, and in any event disappeared before Soviet troops could bring that overwhelming firepower to bear.

The terrain of Afghanistan is heavily mountainous, although the country consists of extensive areas of dry plains, deserts, and 'green zones' of river valleys and vegetation as well. This mountainous terrain strongly influenced the strategy adopted by the Soviets, obliging their commanders to convey troops to an operational area via helicopter or convoy. Whenever possible, they sent troops ahead of the main body or inserted advance parties of troops by helicopter on to high ground to cover those following behind. Yet this of course depended on the availability of such aircraft, required proper planning, and exposed the limited number of helicopters to ground fire, especially rocket-propelled grenades (RPGs) and Stingers (hand-held, ground-to-air rocket launchers).

Close to the larger cities and along frequently travelled roads the Soviets established permanent posts consisting of garrisons of between 15 and 40 troops, who controlled the immediate area, guarded the roads, and guided artillery fire. Owing to their isolation, they could call on help via radio. Some of the most successful Soviet operations involved combined operations, including air assault forces in support of a mechanized ground attack. Helicopters bearing small contingents of these troops would insert them deep in the rear and on the flanks of resistance strongholds to pin insurgents, prevent their withdrawal, destroy their bases, and threaten or cut off their lines of communication. Ground troops would then advance to join up with these heliborne forces and engage trapped Mujahideen, destroying them with superior firepower. Heliborne forces performed best when inserted behind rebel lines within the range of supporting artillery, unless of course their own guns accompanied them. Operations undertaken without artillery support often ended in high casualties for the Soviets.

As guerrillas received and employed new weaponry and developed new tactics, they obliged the Soviets to adapt in turn. For a large conventional force already trying to cope with shifting political circumstances in the country,

Jubilant fighters standing on a downed Mi-24 Hind attack helicopter, the most hated and feared of all Soviet weaponry. (Photo by Chip HIRES/ Gamma-Rapho via Getty Images)

this pressure proved an unwelcome addition to their existing woes, demanding new approaches to seemingly intractable problems in the field. This meant not simply the modification of tactics, but variations to uniforms, weapons, and equipment to suit changing requirements.

The 40th Army comprised a professional cadre of officers and other ranks, but conscripts and reservists formed the bulk of the formation. Like so many American draftees destined for service in Vietnam in the 1960s, they were frequently reluctant or downright unwilling to serve in a war whose purpose they did not understand and in a country about which they knew nothing. The disillusioned Vladislav Tamarov recalled:

> We were drafted at age eighteen. We had no choice. If you weren't in college, if you weren't disabled, if your parents didn't have a lot of money – then you were required to serve. Some young men broke their legs, some paid money [for exemption from service] … (Tamarov 2005: 16)

Those with time on their hands, such as the thousands of soldiers based in rear areas involved in maintenance, logistics, or communications, could easily fall prey to narcotics addiction – heroin of course being readily available in a country where poppies flourished – with predictable effects on morale, though to be fair homesickness and boredom afflicted rear units more than did drug-taking.

Naturally the Soviets possessed elite forces, too, but never in adequate numbers. While ground reconnaissance troops tended to be better trained and of a higher quality than the typical conscript belonging to a motorized rifle unit, the critical shortage of high-quality infantry often led the Soviets to employ reconnaissance personnel in combat rather than in their proper reconnaissance roles. This in turn detracted from the duty of intelligence-gathering on the ground, in compensation for which commanders foolishly relied too heavily on intelligence acquired though aerial reconnaissance, radio intercept, and what little access they had to agents in the field.

These sources did not always yield much of tactical use, and by assigning reconnaissance units to combat duties the Soviets neglected to make best use of their skills and consequently frequently failed to locate Mujahideen forces. The most famous elite forces were the Spetsnaz or 'forces of special designation', highly trained and used in long-range reconnaissance, commando, and special forces functions such as night-time ambushes. They would be helicoptered in and then proceed on foot to the ambush point, there to lie in wait for their unsuspecting quarry.

Most of the infantry carried the 7.62mm AKM assault rifle, while air assault forces carried the 5.45mm AKS-74, the latter inflicting more substantial injury. Soviet heavy weapons included two kinds of rocket launchers: the BM-21 *Grad* ('Hail') and the BM-27 *Uragan* ('Hurricane'). Smaller weapons included the 12.7mm DShK – a heavy machine gun – as well as PTRC guided missile launchers, unguided NURS missiles, SHMELs

Initially, many Soviet troops served in garrison or support roles, with the mistaken expectation that Afghan government forces would bear the brunt of the fighting. (Photo by Alain MINGAM/ Gamma-Rapho via Getty Images)

SOVIET/DRA FORCES AND MUJAHIDEEN STRONGHOLDS, 1980s

ANLF	Afghanistan National Liberation Front (Jabha-i-Najat-Milli Afghanistan)	
HI	Islamic Movement (Harakat-i-Islami)	
HIH	Islamic Party of Gulbuddin Hekmatyar (Hizbi Islami (Gulbuddin))	
HIK	Islamic Party of Mawlawi Yunus Khalis (Hizbi Islami (Yunus Khalis))	
IRMA	Islamic Revolutionary Movement (Harakat-i-Inqilab-i-Islami)	
IUA	Islamic Union for the Liberation of Afghanistan (Ittihad-i-Islami)	
IVOA	Islamic Victory Organisation of Afghanistan (Sazman-i-Nasr-i-Islami-yi-Afghanistan)	
JIA	Islamic Society (Jamiat-i-Islami)	
NIFA	National Islamic Front of Afghanistan (Mahaz-i-Milli-Islami)	
RC	Revolutionary Council of the Islamic Union of Afghanistan (Shura-Inqilabi-i-Itifaq-i-Islami)	

Independent fronts

Airfields
Arms routes
Mujahideen base areas

USSR

U

TURKMEN
SSR

Andkhvoy

Sheberghan   Mazar-e-Sh

BA

Maymaneh

FARYAB
JOWZJAN

Kushka

Qal'eh-ye Now

BADGHIS

BAM

Torkestan Range

Chagcharan

Herat

Koh Range

Kuh

HERAT

Mizan
Valley

GHOWR

AFGHANISTAN

Shindand

URUZGAN

FARAH

Helmand

Tarin Kowt

Farah

Qalat

Khāsh
Desert

ZA

Lashkar Gah

Kandahar

Zabol

Zaranj

NIMRUZ

HELMAND

KANDAHAR

Chaman

Margow
Desert

Rigestan
Desert

Quett

Gowd-e Zereh
Desert

Zahedan

Chagai Hills

Ce
Br
Re

IRAN

Safed

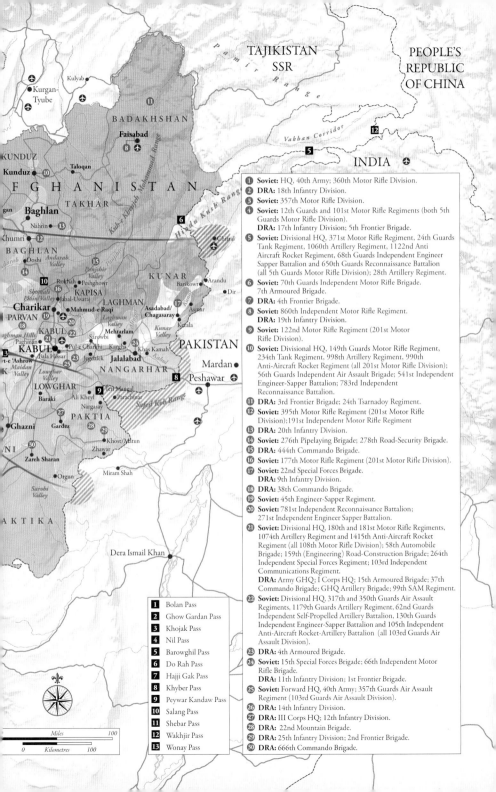

TAJIKISTAN SSR

PEOPLE'S REPUBLIC OF CHINA

Pamir Range

Kulyab

Kurgan-Tyube

Vakhan Corridor

12

BADAKHSHAN

Faisabad **8**

11

INDIA **5**

KUNDUZ

Kunduz **10**

Taloqan

...gan Baghlan

TAKHAR

Nahrin

Kub-e Khwaja Mohammed Range

6

Chitral

Arandu

Dir

...humri **12**

BAGHLAN

Doshi

Andarab Valley

15

Panjshir Valley

Rokhah

Peshghowr

KUNAR

Barikowt

Asmar

Kerala

14

10

KAPISA

16

Jabal-Ussaraj

LAGHMAN

Asadabad/Chagasaray

17

Charikar

Mahmud-e Raqi

Mehtarlam

Kunar Valley

PARVAN

19

18

Paghman

20

Laghman Valley

Sarowbi

...ghman Hills

KABUL

22

Kargha

Khas Kamah

Jalalabad

PAKISTAN

3

KABUL

...te 'Ashrow

Bala Hissar

23

Pul-e Charkhi

Jegdalek

NANGARHAR

Mardan

Maidan Valley

25

Lowghar Valley

8

Peshawar

LOWGHAR

9

Tezi Mangal

Safed Koh Range

Baraki

Ali Kheyl

Nargasay

Parachinar

27

PAKTIA

28

Gardez

Khost/Matun

29

Ghazni

30

Zareh Sharan

Zhawar

Miram Shah

...NI

Orgun

Sarobi Valley

...AKTIKA

Dera Ismail Khan

Hindu Kush Range

1	Bolan Pass
2	Ghow Gardan Pass
3	Khojak Pass
4	Nil Pass
5	Barowghil Pass
6	Do Rah Pass
7	Hajji Gak Pass
8	Khyber Pass
9	Peywar Kandaw Pass
10	Salang Pass
11	Shebar Pass
12	Wakhjir Pass
13	Wonay Pass

Miles 100

0   Kilometres   100

1 **Soviet:** HQ, 40th Army; 360th Motor Rifle Division.

2 **DRA:** 18th Infantry Division.

3 **Soviet:** 357th Motor Rifle Division.

4 **Soviet:** 12th Guards and 101st Motor Rifle Regiments (both 5th Guards Motor Rifle Division).
DRA: 17th Infantry Division; 5th Frontier Brigade.

5 **Soviet:** Divisional HQ, 371st Motor Rifle Regiment, 24th Guards Tank Regiment, 1060th Artillery Regiment, 1122nd Anti Aircraft Rocket Regiment, 68th Guards Independent Engineer Sapper Battalion and 650th Guards Reconnaissance Battalion (all 5th Guards Motor Rifle Division); 28th Artillery Regiment.

6 **Soviet:** 70th Guards Independent Motor Rifle Brigade. 7th Armoured Brigade.

7 **DRA:** 4th Frontier Brigade.

8 **Soviet:** 860th Independent Motor Rifle Regiment.
DRA: 19th Infantry Division.

9 **Soviet:** 122nd Motor Rifle Regiment (201st Motor Rifle Division).

10 **Soviet:** Divisional HQ, 149th Guards Motor Rifle Regiment, 234th Tank Regiment, 998th Artillery Regiment, 990th Anti-Aircraft Rocket Regiment (all 201st Motor Rifle Division); 56th Guards Independent Air Assault Brigade; 541st Independent Engineer-Sapper Battalion; 783rd Independent Reconnaissance Battalion.

11 **DRA:** 3rd Frontier Brigade; 24th Tsarnadoy Regiment.

12 **Soviet:** 395th Motor Rifle Regiment (201st Motor Rifle Division);191st Independent Motor Rifle Regiment

13 **DRA:** 20th Infantry Division.

14 **Soviet:** 276th Pipelaying Brigade; 278th Road-Security Brigade.

15 **DRA:** 444th Commando Brigade.

16 **Soviet:** 177th Motor Rifle Regiment (201st Motor Rifle Division).

17 **Soviet:** 22nd Special Forces Brigade.
DRA: 9th Infantry Division.

18 **DRA:** 38th Commando Brigade.

19 **Soviet:** 45th Engineer-Sapper Regiment.

20 **Soviet:** 781st Independent Reconnaissance Battalion; 271st Independent Engineer Sapper Battalion.

21 **Soviet:** Divisional HQ, 180th and 181st Motor Rifle Regiments, 1074th Artillery Regiment and 1415th Anti-Aircraft Rocket Regiment (all 108th Motor Rifle Division); 58th Automobile Brigade; 159th (Engineering) Road-Construction Brigade; 264th Independent Special Forces Regiment; 103rd Independent Communications Regiment.
DRA: Army GHQ; I Corps HQ; 15th Armoured Brigade; 37th Commando Brigade; GHQ Artillery Brigade; 99th SAM Regiment.

22 **Soviet:** Divisional HQ, 317th and 350th Guards Air Assault Regiments, 1179th Guards Artillery Regiment, 62nd Guards Independent Self-Propelled Artillery Battalion, 130th Guards Independent Engineer-Sapper Battalion and 105th Independent Anti-Aircraft Rocket-Artillery Battalion (all 103rd Guards Air Assault Division).

23 **DRA:** 4th Armoured Brigade.

24 **Soviet:** 15th Special Forces Brigade; 66th Independent Motor Rifle Brigade.
DRA: 11th Infantry Division; 1st Frontier Brigade.

25 **Soviet:** Forward HQ, 40th Army; 357th Guards Air Assault Regiment (103rd Guards Air Assault Division).

26 **DRA:** 14th Infantry Division.

27 **DRA:** III Corps HQ; 12th Infantry Division.

28 **DRA:** 22nd Mountain Brigade.

29 **DRA:** 25th Infantry Division; 2nd Frontier Brigade.

30 **DRA:** 666th Commando Brigade.

(portable, single-shot rocket launchers like RPGs), and mortars. The Soviets deployed various types of aircraft, including MiG23 and MiG27 Flogger fighter-bombers, Su-17 and Su-22 Fitter fighter-bombers, plus Tu-16 Badger medium bombers, and Su-24 Fencer attack aircraft for bombing missions. Mi-8/Mi-17 Hip helicopters transported troops, ammunition, water, and food. Combat helicopters included the Mi-24 Hind attack helicopter, which could provide rapid and accurate firepower for ground attack, convoy escort, and patrolling as well as covering troops with close air support. These proved extremely effective against the resistance and were greatly feared. On the other hand, they suffered from vulnerabilities like all weapon systems, and, as helicopters are most exposed when they are on the ground or hovering over a position, the Mujahideen tended to achieve reasonable success against such aircraft if they caught them in range while landing or disembarking troops.

DRA forces did not enjoy much respect from their Soviet counterparts – and for good reason. Afghan officers could apply for training in a Soviet military college, sometimes within Afghanistan or occasionally in the Soviet Union itself, but they seldom reached a high standard. Apart from volunteers, ordinary soldiers were often acquired by the crude method of virtual kidnapping: troops entered a village and rounded up men of appropriate age. Exceedingly high rates of desertion, sometimes directly into the ranks of the enemy, and numerous instances of DRA soldiers selling their Soviet-supplied weapons to the resistance – including sometimes tanks and armoured vehicles – did nothing to enhance their appalling reputation. Vladimir Tamarov probably reflected the opinion of many of his comrades when he recorded this disparaging impression:

> Frankly, they were lousy soldiers. They tried to stay behind us and were never in a hurry to overtake us. There was nothing surprising about this: many of them, like many

of us, were not in this war of their own free will. We had nothing to lose but our lives, but they were fighting their own people on their own land. Our newspapers depicted them as brave and valiant warriors defending their revolution. There were some volunteers who fought on our side to avenge the deaths of their families murdered by the Mujahadeen. Just as there were those who fought on the side of the Mujahadeen to avenge the death of families killed by our shelling. This is what a civil war is about. (Tamarov 2005: 115)

The Mujahideen

Resistance fighters tended to avoid direct contact with Soviet forces of superior numbers and firepower lest they risk annihilation. Unlike the Soviets, they very rarely fought from fixed positions and if threatened with encirclement simply withdrew. Similarly, in the grand tradition of guerrilla operations, the Mujahideen always sought to achieve advantage through the element of surprise. They benefited enormously from local,

A Pashtun boy, clearly well below military age, conscripted to fight with the guerrillas. Both sides violated international law. (Photo by José Nicolas/Sygma via Getty Images)

intimate knowledge of the ground, possessed years of experience in scouting and reconnaissance and could transmit intelligence on the movement and strength of Soviet units in rapid fashion and across substantial distances by crude but effective means, including signalling devices that the Soviets could neither interpret nor suppress. The Mujahideen were extremely adept at night-fighting, rapid manoeuvre and virtually undetected movement over difficult terrain, and at maintaining a large network of intelligence-gatherers across the country.

Boys as young as 11 or 12 years old fought, carrying Kalashnikovs, together with their fathers and grandfathers. Their motives were various: in rare exceptions they fought simply for money, but overwhelmingly for the sake of defending their country and affirming tribal loyalty. Whatever other motives existed, without question fighting on behalf of *jihad* or holy war compelled most of them. As one fighter explained to Sandy Gall, a British journalist travelling with the Mujahideen:

> Jihad embraces the whole Muslim world. All Muslims are obliged to take part in it by sending money, or demonstrating their support in some other way. Any writer or poet should write only about the Jihad. A merchant should work longer hours to make money for the Jihad. Not to take part in Jihad is a sin. (Gall 1988: 1)

A small minority served in the Mujahideen out of compulsion: fighters simply arrived at a village and threatened to destroy the houses unless men came forward to serve in their ranks, a process which simultaneously prevented DRA forces from adopting the same practice. The number of Mujahideen actively engaged in fighting varied, but an estimated 85,000 served during the final stages of the Soviet occupation in 1988–89, with as many as 110,000 additional insurgents operating on an erratic basis, together with those providing various forms of support, such as logistics, communications, and medical care.

The *mujahid* prided himself on exhibiting bravery in action and often demonstrated a careless disregard for his own life. He was highly motivated, functioned on very little food, moved considerable distances on foot without complaint, generally performed great acts of endurance over rough and mountainous terrain, and adopted a fatalistic attitude that rendered him the most formidable of fighting men. John Lee Anderson, an American journalist who accompanied a unit of Mujahideen, noted:

> Just as they can be harsh when deciding the fate of other people's lives, they can also be stoic when it comes to their own. This stoicism comes out of their culture, in which war enjoys an exalted status, and from their faith in the Islamic idea that after death, a better life awaits. If they are to die, so be it, as long as they do well in battle in the eyes of God. They are mujahideen, holy warriors. They live to make holy war, to kill the enemy, and if necessary be martyred themselves. These are facts they accept. Most of them would have it no other way. (Anderson 2006: 148–49)

In true guerrilla fashion, the Mujahideen possessed no heavy weapons in the form of aircraft or artillery, and thus depended primarily on small arms. Nevertheless, they did employ heat-seeking, Soviet-made, Egyptian-supplied SAM-7 anti-aircraft missiles, though with very poor results. However, at the end of 1986 the rebels acquired American-made Stingers – rocket launchers used in a ground-to-air target role – as well as Blowpipe missiles. They also possessed recoilless mountain guns, mortars, and heavy machine guns, the last known as the DShK, which they pronounced 'dish-kuh'. Some World War II Soviet weapons passed to the Chinese and thence found their way to Afghanistan. The US purchased and supplied largely Eastern Bloc weapons in order to maintain a policy of deniability, thereby obviating Soviet retaliation in some form. With the Saudis matching US funds dollar for dollar, and various other donor nations

Not entirely deficient in heavy weapons, here Mujahideen fighters fire a 122mm artillery piece from the area of Jalalabad, east of Kabul. (Photo by Patrick Durand/Sygma via Getty Images)

including China, Iran, and Britain becoming involved in this illicit arms trade, vast quantities of weapons arrived in Pakistan, where that country's Inter-Service Intelligence (ISI) directly controlled their distribution from near Rawalpindi.

The Mujahideen deployed anti-transport mines such as the 7kg Italian-made TS-6.1, as well as anti-personnel mines, some of which popped up and exploded, while others were activated by the vibrations of footsteps or by radio, or set off by mine detectors. The Mujahideen discovered mines to be even more effective by planting bombs underneath them to increase the strength of the explosion. Mines of various types were pervasive and sometimes severely impeded the Soviets' movement. As Tamarov explained:

> Without minesweepers along, no group ever went into the mountains, no car ever drove off the base, and no transport column ever set out along the road. There were mines everywhere: along the roads, on mountain paths, in abandoned houses. (Tamarov 2005: 74)

OUTBREAK
Insurgency and intervention

In seeking an understanding of the short-term origins of the Soviet–Afghan War, one must look back 20 months to 27–28 April 1978, when a coup staged by a group of Soviet-trained, largely communist army and air force officers overthrew President Daoud, who had himself come to power by deposing the king, his cousin, in 1973. The king, Zahir Shah, had gone into exile in Italy, while Daoud, who had been prime minister from 1953 to 1963, cultivated close relations with the Soviet Union and introduced communists into the government (about half his cabinet). Soon after taking power, however, Daoud began to change his policies, removed communists from his government and purged leftists from the military. When Daoud's interior minister, Mir Akbar Khyber (1925–78), was murdered on 17 April, a large pro-communist demonstration occurred in Kabul, prompting Daoud to order the arrest of communist leaders, including Taraki, the founder of the party, who was detained on 26 April. The coup began the following day, led in particular by Abdul Qadir Dagarwal (1944–2014), Mohammad Aslam Watanjar (1946–2000), Sayid Mohammad Gulabzoy (1951–) and Mohammed Rafie (1946–). Rafie and Qadir belonged to the *Parcham* faction of the Afghan Communist Party, while Gulabzoy and Watanjar came from the *Khalq*

President Mohammad Daoud, who in July 1973 overthrew the king and introduced a pro-Soviet, quasi-Marxist regime, itself replaced by a coup in April 1978. (Photo by Keystone/Getty Images)

wing. Under Watanjar's orders tanks approached the Presidential Palace (known as the *Arg*) with support from MiG-21 fighters and Su-7 fighter-bombers flown from Bagram air base, north of Kabul. The palace guards put up fierce resistance in room-to-room fighting until, at about 4 or 5am on the 28th, the troops reached Daoud and his entire family, whom they murdered. The coup leaders instigated widespread arrests, especially amongst the middle class of Kabul – activists, nationalists, and intellectuals – including two former prime ministers. No serious evidence supports the theory that the Soviets inspired the coup, and while KGB officers in the Soviet embassy appear to have known of the plot beforehand, they were unenthusiastic about it. Rather, it appears to have been the workings of Afghan communists themselves, though clearly it enjoyed Moscow's blessing, for Soviet advisors in the country immediately offered assistance to the new regime.

The coup leaders soon included key civilian political figures from the People's Democratic Party of Afghanistan (PDPA), with Taraki appointed head of state and prime minister, Hafizullah Amin as foreign minister, Qadir as defence minister, and Babrak Karmal as deputy prime minister. In so doing, the regime mixed *Parchami* and *Khalqi* activists, a risky decision that developed into a potentially explosive relationship owing to the fierce antagonism between the two groups. Indeed, within a few months that hostility began to emerge openly. In a meeting on 18 June 1978, which included Taraki, Karmal, and others, an argument broke out that resulted in Taraki ordering Karmal out of the room. In an effort to marginalize his influence, Taraki posted Karmal as Afghan ambassador to Czechoslovakia, along with several of his *Parchami* associates. Other *Parchamis* found themselves sent abroad to fill diplomatic posts, and sensibly refused to return home when the Taraki regime redoubled its purge of the *Parcham* faction – including even coup participants like Qadir and Rafie, who probably owed their narrow escape from execution to their Soviet connections. But many thousands of others enjoyed no such protection and found themselves in the hands of the AGSA (*Afghanistan Gattho Satoonkai Aidara* or Department for Safeguarding the Interests of Afghanistan), the secret police, who imprisoned, tortured, and executed thousands in a campaign of terror meant to intimidate real or potential opponents and to consolidate loyalty around the new regime, now dominated by *Khalqis*.

Accordingly, the infamous Pul-e Charkhi prison in Kabul became notorious for mass killings without a semblance of legal proceedings. The PDPA possessed no real ability to rule the country, since owing to political turmoil and repression it neither controlled nor established an experienced state bureaucracy, nor enjoyed widespread support for its ideas and ambitious plans for restructuring the country along Marxist lines. While employing coercion to instil fear proved effective in protecting the regime, the PDPA's failure to govern once it had secured its power base caused considerable uneasiness in Moscow. The *Khalq* movement instituted radical reforms via decree, with wide-ranging land reforms, including the abolition of peasants' debts to landowners, and a drastic widening of women's rights, including freedom of choice in marriage, abolition of bride-price, and compulsory schooling for girls. The extent of the reforms horrified conservative rural sensibilities, in turn encouraging resistance on religious grounds. Gennady Bocharov, a Soviet journalist, eloquently described the disastrous effect caused by functionaries who obtusely believed they could apply Marxist philosophy in the context of a society living almost as it had 500 years earlier:

> The revolutionary government reached a revolutionary decision: to give the landowners' property to the peasants.
>
> To the peasants, the revolutionary government was as remote and incomprehensible as a government on another planet. The peasant acknowledges only one authority: the *mullah*. And mullahs have been saying for hundreds of years that the land belongs to the master. If you take so much as a handful of the harvest without permission, then Allah's wrath is inescapable. And now this incomprehensible, distant government is saying – take all the land, not just a handful of grain.
>
> The result was that the land lay untilled. Unseeded. Land without hands to tend it. Land running wild …
>
> The revolutionary government decided to introduce co-education in all the schools.
>
> Fathers killed daughters who stepped into a room with boys. Young wives who found themselves in classrooms with strange young men had their throats cut by enraged husbands.

The authorities in Kabul tried to introduce a communist *subbotnik*, or day of voluntary, unpaid labour, on a Friday, the most important day of the week for Muslim prayer. Attendance at the mosques plummeted, resulting in riots. (Bocharov 1990: 57)

Even the gradual introduction of such reforms – including a wide-scale programme of hospital-building and provision of health services to the peasantry for the first time – risked an unpopular reception. In the event, the rapid pace of change guaranteed a hostile response to a regime whose representatives, strangers to the peasantry, journeyed into the countryside to espouse and implement radical ideologies, often at great personal risk. In turn, the regime set upon recalcitrant villages with pathological heavy-handedness, creating a vicious cycle of violence and counter-violence.

Thus, if the new government enjoyed at least some support amongst the military, it possessed precious little from amongst the population as a whole, most of which consisted of small-holding peasant farmers, on behalf

Darul Aman Palace, built in the 1920s for King Amanullah and located about ten miles outside Kabul. It was damaged by fire during the coup in 1978. (François-Olivier Dommergues / Alamy Stock Photo)

Kabuli women attend a literacy course at their place of work in the 1980s. The communist government offered many opportunities for women's education and social interaction. (AFP via Getty Images)

of whom the coup leaders instigated the revolution. By painful irony, the peasants in particular – but some workers, too – rejected the call to Marxism and across the country fomented armed resistance. This movement was encouraged by the poor combat-readiness of DRA forces, which were reeling from a wave of bloody officer purges that together with large-scale desertions rapidly reduced the officer corps to half its normal complement. Some personnel from the lower ranks also abandoned their units, either returning home or joining the resistance, taking their arms and skills with them. But Taraki remained ideologically unshaken; indeed, he strengthened his ties with the Soviet Union when on 5 December 1978 his government signed a treaty that provided for further economic and military aid from Moscow and a 20-year period of 'friendship and

co-operation' between the two countries. When barely a year later the Soviets invaded Afghanistan, they cited the terms of military co-operation stipulated in Article 4 as justifying their action. The treaty thus represented a further overt Soviet effort to bind Afghanistan within its sphere of influence, with military intervention now implicit as a guarantor of fidelity.

On 15 March 1979, owing to brutality committed by *Khalq* activists, a mass revolt erupted in the western city of Herat. Most of the Afghan 17th Division joined the rebel cause, slaughtering untold numbers of government officials as well as some Soviet advisors, who numbered about 550 across the country by this time, and their families. Units loyal to the government moved against Herat and eventually occupied it while the air force bombed the city and the 17th Division. A staggering 5,000 civilians are believed to have died in the onslaught. This extremely brutal approach by the regime made many other soldiers desert to the resistance, some as individuals but others as entire regiments and even complete brigades, reducing army strength by the end of the year to less than half its official strength of 90,000 personnel.

The riots and massacre in Herat triggered an uprising across whole swathes of the country, with opposition preached by mosques and village elders who condemned Marxism as atheistic and anti-Muslim. Religious leaders declared a *jihad*, and as fighting spread across the country the disruption of government business and the harassment of army units and state officials by the Mujahideen rapidly amounted to an intractable problem. Over succeeding months, as the resistance movement gathered pace, there appeared some prospect of its actually overthrowing the regime, reversing the communist revolution and installing an Islamic government in Kabul. In light of the Islamic revolutionary movement's recent ascent to power under the Ayatollah Khomeini (1900–89) in Iran, immediately to the west of Afghanistan, the Soviets naturally wished to prevent this eventuality, not least because of the obvious threat

posed to the key principle underpinning the Brezhnev
Doctrine: that once communism achieved a foothold

in government, the process became irreversible. To the
USSR, any instance of a Marxist 'roll-back' anywhere

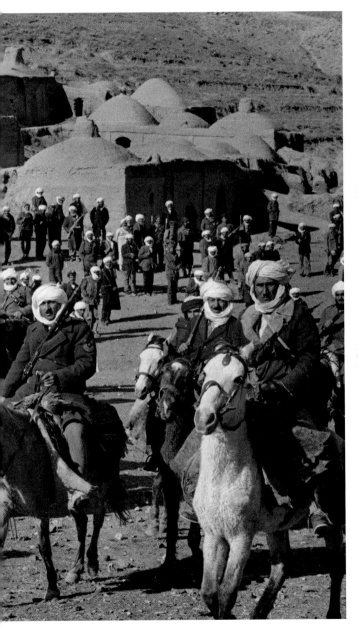

Mounted resistance fighters near Herat. The invasion of a remote and little-known country exposed the inadequacies of the Soviet military machine to cope with a virulent insurgency. (Bettmann/Getty Images)

in the world was anathema on grounds of the potential precedent it set for Eastern Europe, not to mention the Soviet republics themselves.

The Herat uprising caused a serious degree of alarm in Moscow, which began to pay closer attention to military and political events in Afghanistan. If Taraki managed to maintain his grip on power, the Soviet Union could rest fairly easily with a friendly satellite state on its southern borders, a state of affairs critically important in light of the USSR's Muslim republics (Turkmenistan, Uzbekistan and Tajikistan) situated there. Leonid Brezhnev, the Soviet leader, feared that unrest in Afghanistan could spread elsewhere in Central Asia, so threatening the territorial integrity of the USSR. On 17 March, the Soviet Foreign Minister, Andrei Gromyko (1909–89), declared to the Politburo that Afghanistan must not fall from the Soviet orbit, while Aleksei Kosygin, Chairman of the Council of Ministers and later a successor to Gromyko in the Foreign Ministry, stated that the Afghan regime was dangerously inflaming internal opposition and actively attempting to conceal its wide-scale acts of repression from the Soviets. Taraki hysterically and repeatedly requested the intervention of Soviet troops to help maintain order in Afghanistan, but when Kosygin met with him in Moscow on 20 March to outline the Soviet position on Afghan internal affairs, he refused direct military aid: Soviet intervention would worsen matters by inflaming opposition to the regime and arousing international condemnation. The meeting suggests that the Soviets contemplated no long-term strategy to wage war in Afghanistan; it is therefore instructive to examine how and why the Kremlin's *volte face* occurred between March and December 1979.

Matters shifted radically in Afghan politics when in September Taraki and his prime minister, Hafizullah Amin, fell out. The latter, suspecting that Taraki and the Soviets were plotting to oust him, seized Taraki and had him executed on the 14th. This untimely development did not please the Soviets and Brezhnev in particular, who was affronted by his protégé's demise

AFGHANISTAN IS VITNAM OF USSR

under Amin's orders. Significantly, the coup led to nothing less than a fundamental shift in the USSR's attitude and foreign policy respecting its southern neighbour, with the relationship between the two beginning to deteriorate so rapidly that the notion of a Soviet invasion began from this point to become a viable option for the Kremlin.

In the event, Amin's reign of terror – led by the KhAD (*Khedamat-e Ettelaat-e Dawlati* or State Intelligence Agency), as the AGSA was now called – proved worse than Taraki's, with the ruthless pursuit of thousands of genuine and perceived dissidents appearing to be the only answer to Amin's failure to stabilize the domestic situation. The Soviets, angered that this merely exacerbated Amin's internal woes, distanced themselves from his regime, leaving him with no hope of developing closer relations with other powers such as the United States; the US looked particularly unfavourably at the regime after February, when its security forces botched

Afghan students protesting against Soviet intervention after attacking the Soviet Embassy, where they lowered its flag and raised their own in its stead. (Bettmann/Getty Images)

Hafizullah Amin, who had President Taraki, whom the Soviets favoured, killed in September 1979, which in turn triggered Soviet plans for military intervention, which followed in December. (Bettmann/Getty Images)

a rescue attempt to recover the US ambassador in Kabul from the hands of unidentified kidnappers. Besides, the United States, under President Jimmy Carter, found itself so diverted by events in Iran (on 4 November revolutionaries had seized the entire American diplomatic corps from the US Embassy in Tehran) that it paid little attention to Amin's predicament.

Thus, by the autumn of 1979, with the Afghan economy in a downward spiral, the regime rent by political infighting, the country racked by full-fledged civil war and the Mujahideen's increasingly effective opposition looking certain to end in Amin's downfall, the Soviets felt compelled to act. In the months prior to the invasion, Soviet military and KGB advisors toured the country under various pretences to determine the best method of ensuring a rapid subjugation of the country

with a minimum of interference from Afghan forces. But the actual decision to invade did not apparently come until 12 December, during a meeting of the Politburo chaired by Gromyko and attended by Party General Secretary Brezhnev, Andropov, the KGB chairman, and the defence minister, Dmitriy Ustinov (1908–84). The first deployments appear to have begun when the 105th Guards Air Assault Division, under Marshal Sergei Sokolov (1911–2012), shifted troops from Termez in Uzbekistan to Bagram air base, north of Kabul, beginning on 29 November. Late on the evening of 24 December, further contingents from the 105th set down at the civilian airport in Kabul, while other units arrived via heavy Ilyushin and Antonov transport planes at Bagram, the air base at Shindand near Herat, and at Kandahar, the last of the major airfields in the country. In addition, units of the 360th Motor Rifle Division crossed the border near Termez *en route* to the Afghan capital. By launching the invasion around Christmas, the Soviets hoped to lessen the likelihood of any concerted Western objection. Government troops offered no resistance, since they believed the arrival of Soviet forces represented Moscow's desire to uphold Amin in power. As a precaution, Soviet advisors had already removed the firing mechanisms from large numbers of Afghan tanks on the spurious ground that the machines required 'winterizing'.

THE FIGHTING

A war without fronts

While the Soviet–Afghan War may be divided into distinct phases by historians, it is vital to appreciate that the nature of insurgency defies strict adherence to convenient divisions. Set-piece battles, distinct campaigns, and decisive actions indicating the conflict's changing course seldom if ever occur in asymmetric warfare. It is in the very nature of an insurgency, characterized by low- and medium-intensity fighting and the enormous disparity between the protagonists' capabilities, that neither side is capable of inflicting a decisive blow on its opponent via clear-cut encounters. As with all unconventional conflicts, the outcome of the Soviet–Afghan War would depend upon the cumulative effect of years of steadily applied combat power in an attritional contest, in which the winner succeeded in grinding down his opponent through unacceptable losses and a broken will.

Before briefly examining the operational phases of the war a concise discussion of the basic nature of the fighting may be instructive. From the outset fighting took place throughout Afghanistan, with the highest pitch reached in the east, a fact confirmed by the large proportion of refugees and internally displaced Afghans who fled the area over the course of the nine-year conflict. As this region adjoined the Pakistani border, across which the bulk of foreign aid flowed to the resistance over this period, the country's eastern provinces naturally became the focus of particular Soviet attention, with the establishment of a buffer or *cordon sanitaire* their principal objective. To that end, the normal course of fighting did much in encouraging or forcing civilians to abandon the region for the safety and refuge provided by nearby Pakistan. Only later did the Soviets institute a deliberate policy of depopulating vast stretches of territory in a bid to deny the Mujahideen local support in various forms, including food, shelter, and basic intelligence. From the beginning of the war and for most of its course, the majority of the operations conducted by the resistance remained consistent with their limited offensive capability. These consisted of a series of small-scale (albeit seemingly relentless) attacks conducted across most parts of country – the central region of the Hazarajat figuring as a notable exception – in the form of raids, hit-and-run attacks, and moderately sized strikes against Soviet and Afghan regime bases, reconnaissance parties, and small convoys. Bocharov described one such attack against a column of armoured personnel carriers:

Amin's successor, Babrak Karmal, who failed to placate dissent by granting state salaries to thousands of Muslim leaders and providing public money to build mosques. (Photo by Henri Bureau/Corbis/VCG via Getty Images)

[A *mujahid*] clambered out of a hole and opened up with a grenade launcher. The first shot ricocheted off Nikolai's APC and exploded a little way ahead. The next one hit the turret dead-on …

Another missile went under the front wheels and exploded below the first axle. A searing flame burst through from under Nikolai's seat. He felt his entire back to be on fire …

He rolled out onto the body of the vehicle – awful, awful – everything burning all around, no sign of any of the others, just the chatter of automatic fire. He fell to the ground just as two missiles turned the APC into a useless heap of metal. (Bocharov 1990: 36–37)

Two further APCs were hit, killing and wounding several soldiers. Then support arrived in the form of Mi-24 helicopters:

The choppers swooped over the line of foxholes … spitting out pinkish-blue streaks of fire and missiles. Mud, sand, and rocks fountained up, showered down on the trenches, and obscured the sky. The earth groaned

A forest camp in Parachinar, Pakistan. The porous border and safe haven provided by Pakistan proved essential to the survival of the resistance movement. (Photo by AFP via Getty Images)

with explosions and gave birth to dead men. (Bocharov 1990: 40–41)

The Mujahideen proved masters at launching such attacks from places of concealment, as Bocharov recounts further:

> Attacks on Soviet armoured groups were usually carried out without any prior warning. The spooks would emerge out of camouflaged manholes and open fire. Then they would disappear into the depths of their *kirizes*, a network of underground tunnels dug for irrigation purposes, but now serving as perfect bolt holes… They stretched under fields, alongside roads, and underneath villages. *Kirizes* under villages drove the Soviet soldiers mad. One minute you'd have concentrated fire coming from a village, but when you entered it, there wouldn't be a soul to be seen: everyone would have gone to ground in the *kirizes*, and the village would be deserted. (Bocharov 1990: 35–36)

However, these examples should not categorically demonstrate that the Soviet–Afghan War must only be seen in the light of elusive guerrilla attacks followed in their wake by the hammer-blows of a superpower wielding numerically superior numbers and advanced technology, for the resistance did not always hold the initiative. Indeed, as early as March 1980 the Soviets launched their first major offensive with a sweep through the Kunar Valley, which left approximately a thousand Mujahideen and Afghan civilians dead, yet achieved little more than temporarily driving out to other valleys resistance leaders who, in the wake of imminent Soviet withdrawal, resumed their initial positions. Indeed, this scenario strongly characterized the course of the war. The Soviets applied overwhelming force to enable ground troops to establish temporary control of an area after inflicting sometimes sizeable, but seldom crushing and therefore meaningful, casualties on the enemy. These ground troops would then be withdrawn with only a small (and therefore a vulnerable) or no presence left behind, enabling those same opponents to re-establish their former control over territory that Soviet and/or regime forces would have to clear again – a frustrating and costly affair that inevitably favoured the insurgency.

Much of the fighting involved insurgent ambushes directed against patrols and convoys. In the case of the former, the Mujahideen possessed better knowledge of the ground and often struck under cover of darkness, while in the case of the latter, they took full advantage of the limited routes available to Soviet and government

A Mujahideen anti-aircraft position. To the left stands a portrait of Gulbuddin Hekmatyar, leader of Hezbi-Islami, a Sunni fundamentalist group supporting rule by Islamic clergy. (Photo by EPU FILES/AFP via Getty Images)

forces, who found their freedom of movement, even over short distances, hampered by a shortage of roads, particularly paved ones. Regular troops, not trained to confront opponents operating according to radically different doctrine, tactics, and methods of supply and evacuation, could not hope to traverse hundreds of miles of trackless, often mountainous, ground without commensurate support in terms of air power, artillery, and supply. Thus, large formations necessarily depended upon the existing network of rudimentary roads – ironically, most of these constructed by fellow Soviets since World War II.

From the Soviet point of view, the war may be divided into four phases: the first involving invasion and consolidation from December 1979 to February 1980; the second characterized by the Soviets' elusive pursuit of victory between March 1980 and April 1985; the third constituting the period of fighting at its height from May 1985 to December 1986; and the fourth represented by the period of withdrawal from November 1986 to February 1989. These will be examined in turn.

Phase One: December 1979–February 1980

The Soviet invasion amounted to a *coup de main* employing a strategy modelled on that used in their last cross-border intervention during a period of unrest: Czechoslovakia in the spring of 1968. Hostilities began in Kabul on 27 December, when air assault and Spetsnaz forces seized the vital Salang Tunnel and key government and communications points in the capital. There, Colonel Grigori Boyarinov (1922–79), leading special forces, specifically sought out Amin, who had recently relocated from the *Arg* to the Tajbeg Palace in the southern part of the capital. The Soviet assault force duly surrounded and stormed the building, killing Amin and most of his family, but losing Boyarinov in the process. During the assault the city's telephone system shut down after a deliberately timed explosion, and on the evening of the 28th the Soviets used a powerful radio transmitter on their own soil to broadcast a recording of Babrak Karmal announcing Amin's overthrow and naming himself successor. As far as the Soviets were concerned, their seizure of key points across the country, together with the successful installation of Karmal in power, ought to have signalled the practical end of their major military operations in Afghanistan.

Soviet strategy concentrated on a few key objectives. First, the army was to bring stability to the country by protecting the main thoroughfares, placing large garrisons in the major cities, and guarding air bases and points of logistical significance. Once ensconced in these positions, Soviet troops planned to relieve Afghan government forces of garrison duties and redirect DRA efforts against the resistance in rural areas, where the Soviets would provide support on a number of fronts: logistics, intelligence, air power, and artillery. This would enable Soviet forces to take a secondary role in the fighting, thereby both minimizing their contact with the Afghan population and keeping their casualties to an acceptable level. Finally, they planned to strengthen Afghan government forces to the extent that once resistance ceased the Soviets could withdraw their own troops and leave governance and security matters to the 'puppet' regime left in their wake.

The fact that the occupying forces did not anticipate serious resistance may be discerned from their original rules of engagement, which specified that troops were only to return fire if attacked, or to rescue Soviet advisors in insurgent hands. By necessity, these rules rapidly came to be altered owing to the rise in casualties from the very beginning, not least those sustained from urban unrest, the worst of which occurred on 21 February 1980 when approximately 300,000 people crowded the streets of Kabul shouting anti-government and anti-Soviet slogans. The demonstrations continued into the following day when the crowds flowed into the main streets and squares and appeared before the *Arg*, where Karmal made his residence. Thousands laid siege to government buildings,

A Soviet military base in Kabul. The arrogant belief that merely a strong troop presence in cities would cow the insurgency soon proved demonstrably false. (Photo by Patrick ROBERT/Sygma via Getty Images)

threw projectiles at the Soviet Embassy, and killed several Soviet citizens. After the rioters looted scores of shops, overturned and burned cars and set ablaze a hotel, General Yuri Tukharinov, commander of the 40th Army, received orders to block the main approaches to Kabul and stop the demonstrations. This he achieved, but the rising in the capital marked the proper beginning of a resistance movement now extending its remit to oppose foreign forces acting on behalf of Karmal's illegitimate regime.

This left the 40th Army with the unenviable task of defeating the insurgency across the country, a task for which, owing to its original remit of the previous December, it was not properly equipped or trained. In the course of this first phase of the war, that is, the two months from the end of December 1979 to the end of February 1980, the 40th Army had already suffered 245 fatal casualties, largely attributable to regular attacks launched against columns of troops and supplies on the main roads from the Soviet Union. The army responded by establishing mutually supporting guard posts (*zastavas*) at regular intervals that secured the main roads, principal cities, airports, bridges, power stations, and pipelines. These posts observed the insurgents' movements, supported convoy escorts, and could call in air or artillery strikes as necessary. A *zastava* consisted of a dreary guard post with a handful of other soldiers and offered only a modicum of protection. Some held only a dozen men or so, with these often serving in cramped conditions for as much as 18 months without relief, the men suffering from boredom, monotony, bad quality food and water, and virtually no entertainment besides the occasional television. Worst of all, living in such confined and unsanitary conditions, the miserable inhabitants easily spread disease amongst one another and suffered psychologically and physically from the constant threat of insurgent attack. Such posts might sit perched upon inaccessible points, such as atop heights overlooking Afghan villages or routes of supply, so remote in fact as to be incapable of resupply except by helicopter. *Zastavas* regularly came under attack, though none ever fell to the Mujahideen owing to the strength of their structures, not to mention the strenuous efforts made by their diminutive garrisons and their total reliance on the staggering firepower of their heavy machine guns.

By the end of February 1980, 862 *zastavas* dotted the landscape, scattered across Afghanistan, containing garrisons amounting in total to more than 20,000 troops, a fifth of the 40th Army's manpower. This committed troops to a necessary yet static function when the Soviets required substantial numbers actually to pursue and engage the insurgents in order to maintain the initiative or at least to deny it to the enemy. Yet the appetite for such direct engagement did not always materialize to the extent required to meet the insurgent challenge, and for those confined to *zastavas*, appreciating as they did the precarious nature of their existence, the natural instinct for survival prevalent amongst these isolated detachments often induced them to make themselves tolerable to the local population in a sort of 'live-and-let-live' policy. This was unofficially applied all over Afghanistan by small groups of otherwise natural antagonists simply trying to carry on life as tolerably as possible in the midst of a war in which neither party wished to participate. This fact alone shatters the mythology underpinning the popularly held yet simplistic view that every Afghan peasant supported the Mujahideen, and that every Soviet soldier committed senseless acts of brutality, thus rendering himself utterly abhorrent to the inhabitants. There is some truth in both assertions, but the reality – as in all generalizations about war – lies somewhere in between.

Phase Two: March 1980–April 1985

During this period both the 40th Army and the Mujahideen modified their tactics in light of the painful lessons already drawn from the first two months of conflict. No longer would the resistance take on the Soviets in direct confrontations; instead, they turned to guerrilla tactics, with frequent, often small-scale hit-and-run attacks against outposts, convoys, and small units, always seeking to employ the advantage of surprise, particularly in the context of an ambush. The insurgents also planted booby traps and mines along frequently travelled patrol and convoy routes, as well as in abandoned villages. However, the Soviets could sometimes play the game, too, laying ambushes along their opponents' supply routes, as Bocharov witnessed:

> A spray of bullets punctured the camels' bellies and brought them to the ground, clumsily, onto their

fore-legs, roaring with pain. One camel flipped over completely and skidded along the sand on its hump and the boxes strapped to it. The spooks, robbed of cover, sprinted in different directions. One escaped, but they got the other one. Bullets raked through his pelvis just as he got to the lip of the ravine. (Bocharov 1990: 24)

Still, more often than not, it was the Soviets who were ambushed in this way, and to compound their already formidable problems the Mujahideen became increasingly ingenious in their methods of laying mines, as Bocharov recalled with regard to an APC moving between Bagram and Kabul:

An Afghan resistance fighter examines a rocket launcher from a Soviet helicopter shot down in April 1980. (AFP via Getty Images)

They bypassed the combined anti-tank and anti-personnel minefields, and negotiated the most dangerous spot … without incident. Two stray rocket missiles whistled by harmlessly. On one of the sharp turns, the telescopic

antenna that cut through the air above the APC slashed a branch of an overhanging tree. A deafening explosion echoed around the valley, sending stabs of pain through the soldiers' eardrums. Despite its weight of many tons, the APC was flung forward like an empty tub …

There had been a mine fixed to the tree branch, and the antenna had hit it, setting it off. The mine had been put there with APC radio antennas in mind: they were long and flexible, striking branches and rocky overhangs on the mountain roads. (Bocharov 1990: 32)

But the resistance did not rely exclusively on the remote actions of their explosive devices, however numerous and cleverly planted or laid. They supplemented these measures with audacious attacks, as when in the summer of 1980 they bombarded the 40th Army's headquarters, less than 7km (4½ miles) from Kabul, with rockets. The Soviets did not remain idle, striking at resistance positions that they often located from the air and launching the first of many large-scale operations, notably full-scale sweeps of the Kunar and Panjshir valleys between February and April 1980. The last of these marked the largest single Soviet operation since 1945. This dislodged insurgents from a wide area, but only temporarily, while smaller units left themselves vulnerable to Mujahideen attacks of their own, such as in August when the 783rd Independent Reconnaissance Battalion of the 201st Motor Rifle Division fell into an ambush at Kisham in Badakhshan province, near the frontier with Tajikistan, and lost 45 men.

The Soviets struck again in the Panjshir Valley in September 1980, followed by other sweeps against guerrillas in November and from January to February 1981. This region, northeast of Kabul, held particular strategic significance owing to its proximity to the road running north–south that connected Kabul and Mazar-e Sharif through the Salang Tunnel and Pul-e Khumri in Baghlan province. This represented the stronghold of Ahmad Shah Massoud (1953–2001), the best-known Mujahideen leader to emerge during the war. Soviet and DRA forces made nine substantial efforts to clear and hold the Panjshir but never succeeded. Other sizeable operations in 1981 included a largely DRA offensive, which succeeded in securing the Kabul–Jalalabad road near Sarowbi in Kabul province in July. However, regime forces suffered from low morale, performed poorly, and

depended heavily on Soviet co-operation, or shamelessly left the execution of major operations entirely to their patrons. This policy applied equally to the Soviets' fourth major offensive into the Panjshir Valley, in August. This, like the others before it, failed, largely owing to

The Panjshir Valley, whence the Mujahideen continuously threatened the Soviets' vital supply line, the Kabul to Mazar-e Sharif road, as it runs through the Salang Pass. (picassos/Getty Images)

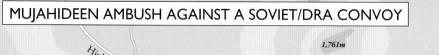

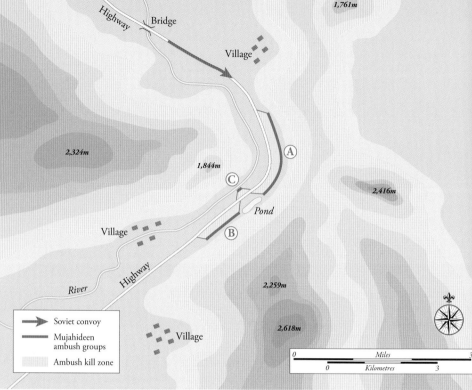

Mujahideen ambush against a Soviet/DRA convoy

One of the most common tactics employed by the Mujahideen was the ambush, by which they made best use of choke-points and high ground to concentrate their forces, strike a target made vulnerable by confined space and poor fire zones, disable or destroy a convoy, seize provisions and retreat before heliborne forces could arrive to support the defenders. In this theoretical scenario shown on the accompanying map, Mujahideen execute an ambush against a convoy of trucks. Such attacks disrupted Soviet and DRA forces' resupply and tied up troops otherwise deployed on strike operations.

This scenario, taking place at about 1pm on a July day, shows a force of Mujahideen setting an ambush against a supply column of 48 trucks, accompanied by an escorting BTR-70 APC at the front and another at the rear; each BTR-70 has a 14.5mm heavy machine gun as its main armament plus a co-axial 7.62mm machine gun, and carries a detachment of seven motor-rifle infantrymen in addition to the three-man crew. The column is moving along a paved section of the 'ring road' linking Afghanistan's major cities and points of supply; the highway is skirted by a river and running through a gorge. The trucks are travelling at 100m intervals; they are carrying food, fuel, oil and lubricants, and ammunition to areas beyond the reach of the supply pipelines upon which the Soviets and their DRA allies depend. The ambush site is located at a particularly vulnerable choke-point where the river runs close to the highway and the hills rise sharply, rendering escape problematical for the convoy's personnel.

The 112-man attacking force is divided into three groups. One group (**A**), 45 men strong with two RPGs and deployed along the bend, is meant to engage the centre of the convoy and the rearguard APC. Another (**B**), also 45 men strong but with three RPGs, is to engage the advance guard and the van of the convoy. A third group (**C**), 22 men with a single RPG, is sequestered in ruined houses beside the river, where they are taking advantage of natural cover that happens to be on the west side of the road and can help bring fire down on any enemy personnel who, perceiving the heaviest fire coming from the east, are likely to exit their vehicles and try to use them for cover. The overall commander is with Group B; none of the groups has radio communication with the other two. The fighters are armed with AK-47 Kalashnikov assault rifles, a few bolt-action Enfield rifles and six RPG-7s, and are hidden in ditches not visible from the road, in positions concealed by camouflage netting and low-growing vegetation on high ground, or in the ruins.

Based on knowledge of the convoy's time of departure and an appreciation of the average speed of a convoy's progress based on previous experience, the Mujahideen commander has made a rough calculation of the convoy's arrival at a given point along its route. His force will attack when the end of the column reaches the northernmost point of Group A's position. Advance warning of the convoy's approach is made available by spotters in the town of the convoy's origin, with the estimated time of arrival in the gorge anticipated with a fair degree of accuracy even without radio communication.

Surprise is likely to reap excellent results: RPGs fired at close range will destroy the APCs to front and rear; the fuel tankers, vulnerable to small-arms fire and grenades, will be attacked and blown up; and the remaining vehicles, carrying food and ammunition, will be stripped of their loads, with any intact trucks driven away to a Mujahideen concentration area – likely to be close by, as Soviet-built trucks could not usually operate off-road. After setting all damaged vehicles on fire and stripping the enemy dead of their personal weapons, the Mujahideen will promptly leave the area, aware that helicopters will soon arrive to ferry away the Soviet/DRA dead and any wounded.

Civilians transporting arms by mule across the Pakistani border to the Afghan resistance. (Photo by ZUBAIR MIR/AFP via Getty Images)

paltry troop levels that rendered holding ground all but impossible for any substantial period. As before, the resistance simply re-established itself across the ground from which the Soviets had temporarily driven it by dint of superior firepower. Resistance casualties certainly mounted, but replacements were always to be found amongst those driven from villages destroyed from the air, living in squalid refugee camps over the border, or preparing for *jihad* in one of the hundreds of *madrassas* (religious schools) in Pakistan, whence thousands of displaced Afghans joined the resistance with the promise of martyrdom for those killed in their holy cause.

In the west, around Herat, Soviet and regime forces engaged in heavy fighting with the Mujahideen in October 1981, with the air base at Shindand, south of Herat, the strong focus of resistance attention. Such actions proved that, despite inhospitable terrain and the great distances across which they conveyed supplies by mule, donkey, camel, and packhorse through the treacherous passes connecting Afghanistan with Pakistan, the Mujahideen could still undertake operations frequently and on a respectable scale. This circumstance was partly rendered feasible by the large exodus of residents from Herat, who were appalled by the regime's suppression of the rising of March 1979 and consequently drawn to the anti-Soviet cause. Further major encounters in and around Herat between the resistance and Soviet and Afghan forces took place in December 1981 and into January of the following year, with continuous, low-level fighting occurring thereafter.

The Afghan regime's ineptitude came to the fore in April 1982 when Mujahideen penetrated Bagram air base and destroyed 23 Soviet and Afghan Air Force aircraft. The following month, another major Soviet–Afghan offensive into the Panjshir occurred, followed by another in August and September, perhaps the largest of all the nine conducted in that area. Both failed to make inroads against Massoud's strongholds despite the enormous scale of the operations. As a consequence of the stalemate reached there, the regime negotiated a ceasefire with Massoud that held from December 1982 to April 1984 on what appeared to be mutually beneficial terms, enabling the Soviets to release thousands of their troops for potentially more successful operations elsewhere. The ceasefire simultaneously provided some relief to Massoud's exhausted forces, and particularly to the gravely stricken local population, whose humanitarian needs the insurgents could not adequately meet in the midst of the Soviet offensive, especially when compounded by the severe winter of 1982–83. Moreover, Massoud's forces had suffered heavily during the offensive, and the ceasefire probably enabled him to recover and regroup before pursuing new operations further north, such as in the Shomali Valley, north of Kabul, where it is thought he struck in conjunction with other commanders, at Soviet positions near Balkh.

In 1983 the Soviets altered their strategy fundamentally, embarking on a deliberate policy of clearing the Afghan population from rural areas and driving them either to seek refuge in the cities, where Soviet or DRA forces exercised more or less total control, or to other, less strategically vital areas within the country or over the border into Iran (which particularly sympathized with and armed the Shi'a minority in Afghanistan) or Pakistan. At the same time, the Soviets continued to conduct major operations against areas where the resistance appeared in concentrated numbers, a painstaking, exhausting, and frequently fruitless undertaking. Owing to poor intelligence, they often focussed their attention in the wrong area of the country, as in the case of the north in the spring of 1983. Here Abdul Qader, known more commonly by his *nom de guerre*, Zabiullah, led as many as 20,000 men and continued to conduct the sort of small-scale operations initiated by him three years before, including attacks, raids, and ambushes in Baghlan, Balkh, and Kunduz provinces, all north or northwest of Kabul. Amongst numerous resistance successes during this phase of the war, the victory achieved in May in Mazar-e Sharif, the principal city of northern Afghanistan, figured prominently. Mazar-e Sharif, whose flat and treeless surroundings rendered guerrilla operations particularly difficult, nevertheless witnessed a bold Mujahideen attack that brought down the civilian airport's control tower.

As was common throughout the country, Zabiullah operated with other local, albeit less powerful, commanders who vied for control of their respective immediate areas, or indeed tried to lay claim to territory well beyond their normal areas of operation. It is vital to appreciate that the Mujahideen did not operate as a unified fighting force with any common objective beyond that of ousting the Soviets from Afghan soil and overthrowing the communist regime, whether headed by Taraki or Amin before the Soviets arrived, or Karmal or Najibullah thereafter. Rivalry between different Mujahideen units, which could consist of merely a dozen to several thousand fighters, sometimes led to open feuds over contested ground; indeed, observers did not rule out the fact that Zabiullah's death, caused by a mine in December 1984, may have constituted assassination rather than a simple vagary of war. If commanders could agree on a common foreign enemy, they also still

maintained an eye on Afghanistan's long-term political future and their place in it.

During the course of 1984, in line with their policy of depopulating regions presumed sympathetic to the Mujahideen, the Soviets conducted a wide-scale bombing campaign in the west, particularly around Herat, driving untold thousands across the border into nearby Iran. In the Panjshir Valley, with the ceasefire over in April, the Soviets opened yet another major offensive that continued into May, with another following in September. The Soviets again employed their new strategy of de-population through a combination of intensive shell fire, regular bombing raids, and mine-laying. In August, the Soviets sought to relieve the siege of the garrison at Ali Sher in Paktia province. There followed further efforts against the resistance in the east from January 1985, with the purpose of clearing areas in order to create bases along the Pakistani border, both to interdict the movement of supplies into Afghanistan

Three Soviet prisoners captured by fighters from the Hezbi-Islami faction of the Mujahideen, held at a camp in Zabul province, January 1982. (Photo by ALAIN FAUDEUX/AFP via Getty Images)

and to weaken the flow of resistance fighters seeking a temporary safe haven in the tribal areas of western Pakistan or in that country's province of Baluchistan further to the south. During this second phase, which ended in April 1985, the Soviets suffered 9,175 fatal casualties – an average of 148 per month.

Phase Three: May 1985–December 1986

During this period Gorbachev, who came to power in March 1985, opened negotiations in an effort to withdraw Soviet forces while simultaneously attempting to reduce the level of casualties during a period when discontent with the war steadily grew. Soviet troops sought increasingly to pass responsibility for making hostile contact with the resistance to their Afghan regime allies, depending themselves more on air and artillery operations, and employing motor-rifle units to support DRA forces both operationally and in terms of morale. As Soviet and Afghan government forces continued to struggle in the east of the country, in June 1985 the resistance struck Shindand air base in the west, destroying about 20 aircraft. Fighting in nearby Herat in July grew so intense that the governor was obliged to leave the city, while at the same time the Soviets launched their ninth and last major offensive in the Panjshir Valley. The DRA regime also continued its efforts: in January 1986 its forces attacked Zendejan in Herat province, inflicting heavy casualties on resistance elements but failing to consolidate its own tenuous control over the region. In the spring, anticipating a Soviet offensive against Zhawar in Paktia province, near the Pakistani border, the Mujahideen reinforced their base there, strengthening their anti-aircraft positions and placing them about 7km (4½ miles) outside their base, complete with defences in depth. They mined the approaches, while small arms, RPGs, mortars, and recoilless rifles covered the area. Communications in the form of field telephones and radios kept the various outposts in contact with one another. The Soviets, in turn, provided one regiment of air assault troops together with 12,000 DRA personnel. Only 800 Mujahideen defended the base at Zhawar, but they received advanced warning of the attack by the presence of two waves of helicopters that approached ahead of the main assault. Air strikes and an artillery bombardment followed, though the attackers could not be certain of the insurgents' positions.

At 7am heliborne troops touched down at scattered landing zones near Zhawar. The defenders shot down two helicopters in the process, but Soviet fixed-wing air support hampered further Mujahideen success and destroyed several of their positions, killing 18 men. Their commander, Jalaluddin Haqqani (1950–2018) and 150 of his men were trapped by debris blocking the cave in which they lay in wait, but by a quirk of fate the carpet bombing that followed cleared the entrance and facilitated their escape. With no answer to the air strikes, the defenders opted to move on to the offensive, thereby remaining close enough to the attackers to avoid fire from the aircraft. Haqqani managed to overrun four landing zones, taking several hundred prisoners in the process – a circumstance that led the Soviets later to alter their tactics to avoid setting down helicopters in the midst of resistance positions that could shower descending aircraft with RPG and machine-gun fire. But the Mujahideen could do no more: Soviet and Afghan forces managed to outflank Haqqani's position, forcing his men to fall back, and as reinforcements continued to appear around Zhawar, the resistance declined to maintain what amounted to an impossible defence and scattered.

DRA troops held Zhawar for a few hours but unaccountably neglected either to carry off the arms and ammunition that remained for the taking, or even to destroy them. Likewise, they made a feeble attempt to destroy the caves with explosives, while their opponents, refusing to withdraw without registering a final act of defiance, fired rockets at regime forces as if to signify the hollow victory that Zhawar represented for Kabul. Indeed, within a few weeks the base returned to operational status, garrisoned once again by resistance fighters, whose losses in the defence of Zhawar amounted to 281 killed and 363 wounded, with government forces suffering similar losses. As hitherto commonly practised, though of course utterly forbidden by international law, the Mujahideen executed all of the officers they captured and compelled the soldiers to submit to two years' manual labour in rear logistical areas, with the promise of release after serving their time. Zhawar demonstrated that the resistance could not, in fixed positions, hold out against the concentrated firepower of Soviet and DRA forces. Nevertheless, in turn, although outwardly successful, their opponents could not muster the numbers to hold positions seized in the operation.

Camp near Zhawar in Paktia province, May 1985, with captured Soviet armour in the background. (Photo by Philippe FLANDRIN/ Gamma-Rapho via Getty Images)

The capture of the major resistance base at Zhawar in spring 1986 signified a welcome development for regime forces in an otherwise frustrating campaign against opponents who proved exceedingly difficult to pin into position, and who seldom entered an engagement except where the ground, weather, numbers, or other factors played to their advantage. But successes such as Zhawar

failed to conceal the fact that Soviet and DRA forces could rarely produce more than a temporary impact over a limited area before insufficient numbers and military priorities elsewhere obliged their withdrawal to their bases of operation. Thus, taking ground posed comparatively few problems for conventional forces enjoying vastly superior firepower; holding that ground, on the other hand, required a far greater commitment in manpower than the Soviets were prepared to make. Withdrawal inevitably left in its wake a vacuum that the Mujahideen quickly filled.

In the south, the regime largely controlled Kandahar, but it could never hold down the region permanently against resistance units under such talented commanders as Haji Abdul Latif, or the numerous other smaller rebel factions formed and held together by tribal loyalties or clustered around a particularly charismatic leader. If fighting in southern Afghanistan, particularly in and around Kandahar, tended to manifest itself in skirmishing, in contrast to the larger-scale operations conducted in the east by Soviet troops, it nonetheless occupied the attention and energy of regime forces for years. The absence of set-piece battles, co-ordinated campaigns, and great sweeps may suggest a sense of tranquillity, but nothing could be further from the case. Low-intensity warfare by definition does not yield heavy casualties in the short term (there is no Somme, El Alamein, or Stalingrad), but gradual, mounting losses inflicted by the Mujahideen slowly ground down Soviet morale, encouraging the cycle of atrocity and counter-atrocity so characteristic of irregular warfare. Indeed, both sides committed barbarities against each other until they became commonplace. The Soviets sometimes cold-bloodedly dispatched prisoners by dropping them from helicopters after interrogation, or simply shot them in the head. The resistance, for its part, sometimes tortured its captives by means of castration, disfigurement, or skinning alive. A lingering death could be created by securing the prisoner to pegs planted in the ground, his death coming slowly under a baking sun, or more swiftly via beheading.

Vladislav Tamarov, the young Soviet conscript quoted earlier, observed some of the more common varieties of atrocity committed by both sides:

> I saw houses burned by the Mujahadeen, as well as disfigured bodies of prisoners they'd taken. But I saw other things too: villages destroyed by our shelling and bodies of women, killed by mistake. When you shoot at every rustling in the bushes, there's no time to think about who's there. But for an Afghan, it didn't matter if his wife had been killed intentionally or accidentally. He went into the mountains to seek revenge (Tamarov 2005: 116).

Often the combatants simply refused to offer quarter, as Tamarov recalled in the case of one *mujahid* with his arms raised above his head in token of surrender.

> According to the rules of war, I should have taken him prisoner. But there were no rules in this war. I had no

An Afghan woman amidst her ruined village. Soviet bombing designed specifically to de-populate the countryside forced civilians into more easily controlled urban areas. (Photo by Peter Turnley/ Corbis/VCG via Getty Images)

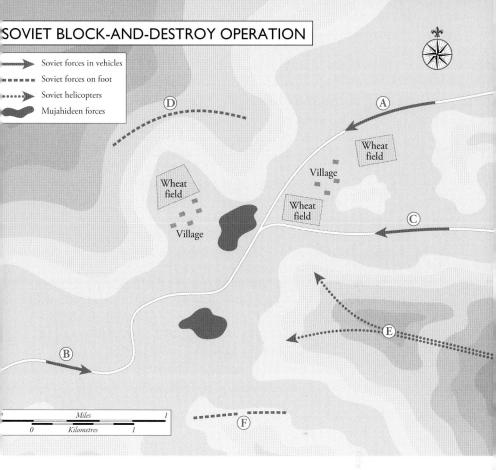

SOVIET BLOCK-AND-DESTROY OPERATION

Soviet forces in vehicles
Soviet forces on foot
Soviet helicopters
Mujahideen forces

A
D
Wheat field
Village
Wheat field
Wheat field
Village
C
B
E
F

Miles   1
0   Kilometres   1

Soviet block-and-destroy operation

As shown on the accompanying map, Soviet block-and-destroy operations involved dispatching forces to areas known to contain sizeable concentrations of Mujahideen, blocking their retreat before engaging and destroying them; several independent resistance forces would sometimes gather in one place to plan and execute a major operation. In this case, Soviet ground troops operating out of tracked BMP-1 infantry fighting vehicles will comb through the villages, killing or driving out into the open any Mujahideen forces taking refuge among the local population, while various other combat elements, including air assault troops inserted by helicopter, will press the enemy from various directions, denying escape routes wherever possible. It is very unlikely that the Soviet forces will take prisoners; quarter was seldom given.

To this end, three motorized rifle companies – (**A**), (**B**) and (**C**) – together totalling about 300 men, will converge on Mujahideen positions from three directions by road.

A mountain-rifle battalion (**D**), about 600 men strong, will arrive in BMP-1s, then advance across the heights towards a village below that is known to provide aid to the enemy.

Meanwhile, 12 Mi-24 Hind helicopter gunships (**E**) will approach to engage the enemy while they remain in open ground; they will arrive in two six-ship groups, both flying in a pattern-eight, one group behind the other. They will approach at low altitude, using flares to distract any infra-red missiles. At 7,500m from their target they will attack with rockets from an altitude of about 80m, but will remain beyond 1,500m so as to avoid enemy machine-gun fire.

To the south, poised on a rocky outcrop lies a 90-man air assault company (**F**), inserted by air using Mi-8 Hip helicopters and carrying BM-12 rockets, 82mm mortars, AK-74s, and RPK-74 light machine guns. Their mission is to deploy on heights overlooking a Mujahideen position and prevent the escape of any enemy forces driven off by other elements of the Soviet offensive.

If properly co-ordinated, swift Soviet deployment by road and air, including the use of small numbers of tanks, BMPs or BTRs – with or without accompanying dismounted troops – stands to provide the Soviets with decisive results.

choice – there were only three of us, and we didn't know how many of them were left. To this day, I remember the fear in his eyes; it was so strong, that it was hard for me to take aim. All I could do was close my eyes and pull the trigger. (Tamarov 2005: 126)

The Soviets, far from pursuing a 'hearts and minds' campaign in order to encourage the population's sympathies with the government in Kabul, committed atrocities with shocking regularity against villages suspected of aiding the resistance or in retaliation for ambushes. Such ruthless, counter-productive acts certainly forced out vast numbers of the inhabitants – denying the Mujahideen some of the rural support so vital to their operations – but the short-term advantage thus gleaned by shifting populations and destroying farmland by sowing aerial mines or bombing paled in significance against the numbers of survivors thus driven into the hands of the guerrillas. Thousands joined local guerrilla groups, while most fled across the Pakistani border to join the resistance at its base in Peshawar before returning, trained, armed, bitter, and vengeful. A young refugee Afghan boy of about eight graphically related an account of the Soviets arriving in his village:

> The mujahideen went back to the mountains. They [the Russians] came in our direction. We were all in bed. They broke down the door and came in. The door was smashed. We were all frightened and jumped up. My brother didn't get up but they forced him to stand up. They shot my father and my brother. They lifted me up and wounded me with their bayonets ... I lay down and cried. I was sad because my father had been killed. My father was dead and was lying on the ground. They took us outside. I saw lots of people had been taken out of their houses into the alleyways and killed. We went to the bazaar. The shops, the shops had been burnt. People had been killed. Everywhere women had been killed, men had been killed, even boys ... They didn't leave a single one alive. (Quoted in Gall 1988: 1)

Appreciating at last that such counter-productive methods only galvanized the population's defiant stance, and increasingly aware that their military prospects were in decline, in the summer of 1986 the Soviets eased their campaign of driving civilians out of rural areas in favour of seeking to secure their co-operation with, if not allegiance to, the regime in Kabul. This very belated, cynical policy yielded few dividends from a people marginalized by brutality and the forced conscription of their menfolk into the ranks of the DRA forces, as well as by the presence of foreign troops supporting a deeply unpopular regime. Thus, the fighting merely continued as before. On 6 July, the resistance conducted a co-ordinated and successful attack against an enormous Soviet convoy near Maymaneh, the capital of Faryab province near the Turkmenistan border, while in August the Soviets, supported by Afghan security forces, conducted substantial sweeps into the Lowghar Valley. On the 26th of the same month, the Mujahideen set off massive explosions near Kabul when they fired 107mm and 122mm rockets into ammunition dumps at Kargha. Arriving to secure the area and the nearby town of Paghman, Afghan government forces met heavy opposition that left the area in ruins after a fierce engagement. At about the same time, intense fighting took place in Herat.

During this third phase of the war the Soviets made more substantial use of special forces in the form of Spetsnaz and reconnaissance units, which sought to interdict the transfer of weapons, ammunition, and supplies destined for the Mujahideen from Pakistan. However, the frequency of contact during this particularly bloody period of the conflict cost the Soviets 2,745 personnel killed, an average of 137 a month. These elite units performed well, and their deployment in greater numbers demonstrated the Soviets' eventual recognition that such forces could fulfil the pressing operational need for highly mobile, highly trained, specialist troops

A soldier of the army of the DRA, an institution plagued by internal divisions, lack of motivation to serve the Marxist government, and high rates of desertion. (DOUGLAS E. CURRAN/AFP via Getty Images)

conversant with the tactics of counterinsurgency. But the Spetsnaz and other elite forces never accounted for more than 15 per cent of Soviet combat power and simply could not sustain the extremely punishing levels of continuous deployment imposed on them. Indeed, even as the number of special forces personnel reached its height in Afghanistan, 15,000 other troops withdrew in the summer of 1986, in line with Gorbachev's decision to bring home all field personnel by early 1989.

Phase Four: November 1986–February 1989

With the war clearly going badly and the Soviets now committed to withdrawing, they were keen to bolster the new president, Mohammad Najibullah (1947–96), the brutish former head of the vicious KhAD. They were particularly enthusiastic about Najibullah's 'Policy of National Reconciliation', a plan to reconcile the government with moderate political and religious leaders of non-communist persuasion while simultaneously strengthening the numbers and capacity of Afghan forces and security personnel, in recognition of the somewhat disconcerting fact that the regime would soon depend largely upon its own wits and resources to defeat the insurgency after final Soviet withdrawal.

Soviet forces naturally continued to support the efforts of the DRA, but by now commanders sought to preserve the lives of men soon to be dispatched home. Part of this process included increasing attacks by air, with heavy bomber strikes originating from the Soviet Union against Mujahideen positions around Faisabad, Jalalabad, and Kandahar, which ground troops had already evacuated. The Soviets also unsuccessfully launched raids against insurgent rocket batteries shelling Kabul on a regular basis, and, as their last forces were withdrawing, aircraft hit the Panjshir Valley in an effort to keep Massoud's forces distracted there. But in this fourth and final phase the Soviets largely occupied themselves with completing their withdrawal, which they carried out in two stages:

Difficult and varying terrain rendered many Soviet armoured vehicles unsuitable or requiring adaptation. Infantry within adopted static tactics, and the vehicles' fireports severely limited visibility. (Photo by Robert Nickelsberg/ Getty Images)

between May and August 1988 and from November 1988 to February 1989.

Apart from Soviet troop withdrawals, this phase of the war is notable for two other features: the introduction into resistance arsenals of the Stinger ground-to-air missile, whose effectiveness, though often exaggerated, nevertheless manifested itself in the serious blow it inflicted on Soviet air power; and the increasing frequency of raids conducted by the Mujahideen over the Soviet border.

With respect to the Stinger, Bocharov witnessed at first hand the weapon's lethality against helicopters:

> Suddenly, the chopper shuddered, as though it had collided with something, pitched over to one side, and seemed to halt in midair. Then, describing an imperfect parabola, it seemed to head back for the ground. But it wasn't flying back – it was falling, falling like a stone. A [missile] had pierced its stabilizer, wrecked the metal, and set the fuselage on fire. The pilots made desperate efforts to pull out, but it was useless. The chopper, with its full load of wounded, roared toward the ground. (Bocharov 1990: 43)

Observers dispute the number of Soviet aircraft downed by the Stinger, but it may well have accounted for hundreds. At the very least it induced pilots to fly at higher altitudes, attracting to themselves the derisive appellation of 'cosmonaut' – a contemptuous reference to their staying out of range.

Although the Mujahideen inflicted only small degrees of damage in cross-border raids into the Soviet Union's Central Asian republics, they palpably established the fact that not only had the Soviets failed to bring the insurgency under control, but also the resistance could penetrate enemy territory almost at will, such as during an operation conducted about 20km (12½ miles) north of the Amu Darya River in April 1987, when insurgents bombarded a factory in Tajikistan with rockets.

As before, though, such small-scale operations functioned in tandem with much larger engagements, such as the renewed heavy fighting that took place in Herat on 7 April, when encounters in the streets resulted in over 50 casualties inflicted against Soviet and DRA personnel. The following month the Soviets launched an operation specifically intended to relieve the besieged garrison of Ali Sher in Paktia province. Although a Soviet success, the Mujahideen struck back to ensure their opponents did not establish a permanent presence in the area, forcing them out in mid-June. The following month, on 27 July, particular trouble erupted in the south (never a tranquil place, even before the Soviet invasion), when a Mujahideen missile brought down a plane containing senior Soviet and Afghan officers while attempting a landing at the airport in Kandahar. At about the same time, the small Soviet garrison at Bamiyan abandoned the city after holding off a Mujahideen attack. The resistance stepped up its campaign of terror in Kabul when on 9 October it planted a car bomb that killed 27 people, one of many urban terrorist attacks launched by the resistance in towns and cities across Afghanistan.

Further proof of the Soviets' inability to hold much more than the ground on which they stood became evident after the successful relief of the besieged city of Khost, in which 18,000 troops, of whom 10,000 were Soviets, succeeded in re-opening the road between Gardez and Khost to convoys between November and December 1987. The Soviets eventually abandoned these positions

Soviet airborne troops cross the border in February 1989 near Termez, which served as headquarters for 40th Army operations in Afghanistan. (Photo by VITALY ARMAND/AFP via Getty Images)

at the end of January 1988, in another striking example of their inability to secure even positions of significant strategic value while burdened by other pressing demands on troops and supplies. Shortly thereafter, as part of their policy of withdrawal, the Soviets left Kandahar to an uncertain future under tenuous DRA control.

With Soviet forces evacuating the south of the country, activity continued in other regions, where resistance fighters, emboldened by their opponents' withdrawal, struck in Kabul on 27 April 1988. A truck bomb exploded during the tenth anniversary of the communist takeover, killing six and wounding several times more. Bombs planted in vehicles formed only a single aspect of the Mujahideen's renewed attacks in Kabul. On 9 May they fired rockets into the city, killing at least 23 civilians, with many more similar attacks to follow over the coming months. Such acts of terror failed to weaken the regime's grip on the city, but they exposed in stark terms the futility of the authorities' efforts to protect the inhabitants from indiscriminate violence and thus to demonstrate a capacity to maintain security even within urban areas, much less within the seat of government itself. In short, by operating in and around Kabul seemingly at will, the Mujahideen sought to underline the inevitability of the regime's downfall.

In May and June 1988, renewed fighting between local resistance forces and government troops took place in Kandahar, a city no longer garrisoned by Soviet troops, but with no decisive results. Still, the Mujahideen succeeded on 17 June in seizing Qalat, the capital of Zabul province. As the first such city to fall to the resistance, Qalat was a place of symbolic importance. The victory proved short-lived, however. Straddling the main road between Kabul and Kandahar, Qalat enjoyed a level of strategic significance which the regime could not ignore lest its retention by the Mujahideen signal the general defection of other towns and cities across the country. As such, DRA forces took particular pains to retake the city four days later.

All told, this last phase of the war cost the Soviets 2,262 fatalities, with an average of 87 deaths per month.

The funeral for five Afghan children killed in Kabul while playing football, reportedly victims of a Chinese-made rocket launched by Mujahideen forces. (Photo by Robert Nickelsberg/Getty Images)

Conclusions

An analysis of the operational record of the conflict reveals that the Soviets completely failed to accept that their doctrine and training ill-suited them for the type of war into which they plunged themselves. Fully capable of undertaking operations on a grand scale and in a conventional context, apart from their special forces Soviet troops were not armed, equipped, or trained for a platoon commander's war, which entailed locating and destroying small, elusive, local forces which only stood their ground and fought when terrain and circumstances favoured them, and otherwise struck quickly before rapidly melting away. There were no fixed positions, no established front lines, and rarely any substantial bases of operation for the insurgents. Whereas the Soviets could perform extremely well at the operational level, complete with large-scale all-arms troop movements, this could not be easily adapted to circumstances on the ground – where the war was a tactical one, in which Soviet tactics did not conform to the requirements of guerrilla warfare. Soviet equipment, weapons, and doctrine suited their forces well for a confrontation on a massive scale on the northern European plain, a context in which they were confident in employing massed artillery to obliterate NATO's defensive positions before driving through the gaps created to crush further resistance and to pursue the remnants of shattered units.

Soviet tactics simply did not accord with their opponents' fighting methods. No benefit accrued by massing artillery to carry out a bombardment of an enemy who seldom concentrated in large numbers and who dispersed at will, reforming elsewhere for the next ambush or raid. Soviet conscripts and reservists could dismount from a personnel carrier and deploy rapidly for the purpose of laying down suppressive fire on an enemy unit or sub-unit of like composition, but the tactics and standard battle drills of the typical motorized rifle regiment failed to match the attacks of a highly mobile, fluid enemy who refused to fight on terms consistent with Soviet doctrine. Air assault and Spetsnaz forces learned to adapt their tactics to meet the demands of a guerrilla war,

and in this regard they achieved some success. But the level of innovation required to defeat such a wide-scale insurgency proved beyond the means of Soviet forces as a whole, and thus must be seen as one amongst many factors that doomed them to ultimate failure.

A destroyed Soviet tank at Ali Kheyl, near the Pakistani border. Highly mobile, RPG-armed insurgents made short work of armour inadequately supported by infantry. (Photo by ZUBAIR MIR/AFP via Getty Images)

The Soviets laboured under the illusion that because the heavy application of military force had succeeded in the past, it was bound also to succeed in current operations. Important precedents existed to support this view, including the numerous campaigns conducted against independence movements as long ago as the Russian Civil War and into the 1920s, when Bolshevik forces put down revolts in the Ukraine, Central Asia, the Transcaucasus, and even the Far East. During World War II – quite apart from the herculean efforts first to oust the Germans from home soil and then to drive on Berlin – Soviet forces quashed serious opposition from Ukrainian and Belorussian nationalists, some of whom carried on the struggle after 1945. After all this, and when their forces easily put down the risings in East Germany,

Hungary, and Czechoslovakia, the Soviets could be forgiven for thinking that their might stood invincible against all foes, conventional and unconventional alike.

Afghanistan exploded this fallacy. Even when they adapted to new circumstances, the Soviets failed to deploy sufficient numbers of forces to fulfil their mission. They could not possibly hope to defeat the insurgency when spread across such a vast area. The defence of bases, airfields, cities, and lines of communication alone committed the bulk of Soviet forces to static duties when circumstances demanded unremitting strike operations against the insurgents, thereby maintaining the initiative and obliging the resistance to look to their own survival in favour of attacks of their own. Soviet regiments, companies, and platoons routinely stood under-strength, with regiments often down to single battalion strength and companies little more than oversized platoons. Much of this occurred despite the large biannual troop levies, which certainly furnished the men required, but whose numbers needlessly dwindled enormously due to poor field sanitation practices and inadequate diet, both of which contributed to the widespread dissemination of disease throughout the armed forces. A staggering one-quarter to one-third of a typical unit's strength was diminished by amoebic dysentery, meningitis, typhus, hepatitis, and malaria, leaving actual field strength woefully low and so operationally compromised that commanders deemed it necessary to create composite units on an ad hoc basis.

In assessing the tactics and fighting capacity of the 40th Army, one is struck by the generally poor performance of its regular units. As discussed earlier, they were trained to fight NATO forces on the plains of central Europe, with a strict adherence to orthodox formations and methods of attack. This obliged Soviet infantry to remain close to their armoured vehicles as they advanced down valleys in which the Mujahideen took full advantage of the ground, much of it familiar to them. Performance improved amongst Soviet units as they examined their mistakes, but the problem of understrength units regularly dogged their efforts. Little could be done to counter the continuous drain on their morale caused by the anxiety imposed by the constant threat of attack by guerrillas who sought out the Soviets' vulnerabilities by day, but especially by night, causing physical and mental exhaustion. The war required immense physical efforts to make contact with an elusive opponent, but many Soviet soldiers lacked the stamina to cross the great distances necessary to come to grips with their enemy, not least across inhospitable terrain. Their training and equipment proved inadequate, and security and intelligence, particularly at the tactical level, proved poor to the extent that even when attempting to surround groups of insurgents, Soviet troops often failed to close the ring, thus allowing the enemy to escape through gaps or otherwise fight their way out. Overly confident in its fighting capacity, an attitude perhaps reinforced by a reputation of military invincibility earned as a consequence of the Red Army's extraordinary performance in World War II, and with no combat experience acquired since that time, the 40th Army found itself the victim of breathtaking hubris. Ill-trained for the type of warfare in which it engaged and incapable of achieving the unrealistic aims set for it by Moscow, it launched into the fray regardless.

Soviet aircraft waiting to transport the last troops out of Kabul during their ignominious withdrawal in February 1989. (Photo by Eric BOUVET/Gamma-Rapho via Getty Images)

THE WORLD AROUND WAR
A glimpse of rural Afghanistan

Afghanistan has a turbulent, often violent, history. It is a land of hardened, brave, highly independent peoples who have adapted to a harsh and unforgiving climate and maintain a fierce sense of independence, an unshakable religious faith, and a deep sense of loyalty to family and clan. Many of these features stem from the country's long association not merely with inter-tribal strife – certainly an historically prominent and pervasive feature of Afghan life in its own right – but with foreign intervention and war, pre-dating even Alexander the Great's incursion in the 4th century BC. Since this time every successive invader, whether Persian, Mongol, Briton, or one of many others besides, has encountered intractable resistance and often military disaster. In light of all this, perhaps unsurprisingly, the Afghan character, if often generalized and stereotyped, has followed a familiar pattern stretching across the centuries – particularly in its martial qualities, as one Western observer noted during the height of the Soviet occupation:

> Afghans are a tough people who can live on bread and goat's milk, and most who have known them have commented on their extraordinary personal dignity and love of freedom. The Afghans believe that the greatest of all virtues are revenge and hospitality. They never forgive

an injury, yet paradoxically they do not turn away a guest even if he is a tribal or personal foe. These qualities are particularly associated with the Pushtuns [sic]. The romantic image is of a tall, bearded tribesman striding along a rocky path with a rifle on his shoulder and a fierce glint in his eyes. His land is everything and his home, with its thick mud walls, stout gates, and watch towers at the corners, is his castle. His prestige and honor depend on his ability to defend them against a foreign invader, against another valley – or against another branch of his family. It sounds gloriously heroic, but from the cold view of politics it amounts to ordered anarchy. (Bonner 1987: 25–26)

The literal meaning of 'Afghanistan' is simply 'Land of the Afghans', a term which deceptively suggests that its people compose a single ethnic group, a circumstance which could not be further from reality. In fact, Afghanistan, situated in the heart of Central Asia, stands within a crossroads of major geographical and cultural regions, with Iran immediately to its west and the Indian sub-continent to its east, with Pakistan sharing a lengthy border both to its east and south, thus rendering Afghanistan land locked. Even the Far East is not too distant, for the Pamir Mountains extend like a finger far into China's Sinkiang province. In this very brief sketch,

An Afghan praying in a refuge camp for internally displaced people in Paktia province. The war created the world's greatest refugee crisis since 1945. (Photo by Robert Nickelsberg/Getty Images)

space precludes discussion of the country's varying topography and climate, but one may soon acquire an impression of its formidable size via simple comparison. Afghanistan is about 652,860km² (252,070 square miles), larger than France and roughly the size of the state of Texas, with extremely varying terrain. It is dominated by mountains and deserts, relatively few major rivers and numerous narrow mountain valleys. The country consists of harsh, inhospitable terrain that renders living hard, demanding considerable labour on the land.

Indeed, when the war began only about 12 per cent of the land was under cultivation annually, owing to shortages of water. Land is irrigated where possible, but dry farmed land produces wheat and barley, although never in great abundance. While pre-war Afghanistan certainly ranked high amongst the poorest countries of the world, its people did not suffer from acute hunger, for its soil, though hardly rich, sustains a variety of basic foodstuffs including corn, rice, sugar beets, sugar cane, oilseed, vegetables, nuts, and fruit, all supplemented with meat in the form of lamb, beef, and chicken. Farmers graze principally sheep and goats, and employ water buffalo as plough animals, or the yak in the Pamir Mountains. Of a pre-war population of about 14 million – although this figure is disputed, with up to 18 million claimed – 85 per cent of Afghans tilled the land or served in agriculturally related work, enabling this relatively small population to survive with such a diminutive area of cultivated land at its disposal. Having said this, the shortage of arable land was naturally worsened by the mines sown by the Soviets and the severe destruction wrought on the country's centuries-old irrigation systems.

Afghanistan is a land rich in horses, with hardy pack horses capable of carrying loads of up to 90kg (200lb) at about 5½km/h (3½mph), while donkeys perform almost as well, conveying about 68kg (150lb) at 4km/h (2½mph). Villagers often transport heavy loads on donkeys to town bazaars, selling what they can and returning bareback if possible. Mules are also used as pack animals, together with camels, the latter irritable and bad-tempered beasts having long since appeared in Afghanistan thanks to Central Asian nomads, who favoured the one-humped dromedary. Whatever their variety, camels in Afghanistan can carry loads of 180kg (400lb) in the plains and 135kg (300lb) in the mountains.

Introduced into the country in the mid-7th century, Islam – overwhelmingly of the Sunni faith – plays a fundamental part in daily life and politics and, in the absence of a proper national identity, supplies the only single unifying factor throughout the country. An American journalist visiting Afghanistan in 1985 observed part of the daily religious routine:

> With the distant sound of a priest intoning the call to prayer and the crowing of cocks, the room came to life. The men … performed their morning ablutions, washing their faces, ears, arms, feet, legs, and genitals. Only then did they say their morning prayer, the first of the five that a Muslim must say every day. It was still early. The first prayer comes just before dawn. Some of the men went back to sleep. Others sat next to the lamps, which had been relit, and silently read from the Koran. Some of their copies were only palm-sized, to be carried in a man's pocket near his heart. Others were the size of a paperback book. (Bonner 1987: 7)

A Kabuli spice merchant. Urban populations swelled enormously due to internal displacement, with refugees seeking safety in places like Kabul, Herat, Jalalabad, and Kandahar. (Photo by DANIEL JANIN/AFP via Getty Images)

Apart from the Muslim faith, the dominant characteristics of the Afghan people are their ethnic diversity, overwhelmingly rural pattern of life, and dearth of education. When the war began illiteracy ran at 90–95 per cent, since as a basically agrarian economy, the ability to read and write offered little advantage to village-dwellers, who in any event seldom had access to schooling. In terms of ethnicity, the Pashtuns form the largest group, representing at least 40 per cent of the population. Second are the Tajiks, making up approximately 20 per cent. The next three largest ethnic groups are all about the same proportion, being the Hazaras, the Uzbeks, and the Aimaq. Yet in this multi-faceted society there are many other groups, including Turkmens, Kazaks, Wakhis, Baluchis, Qizilbash, Nuristanis, and Kyrgyz, plus small minorities of Hindus, Sikhs, and Jews. In all, Afghanistan is composed of at least 20 ethnic groups. Before and during the war these groups largely inhabited their own villages that surrounded towns of more mixed ethnicity, but in general ethnic integration in the countryside was rare. In the decades since Soviet occupation these trends have remained largely unchanged.

As the largest ethnic group in the country, the Pashtuns numbered about 6.5 million people when the war began. As a people, the Pashtuns are divided into two separate confederations of tribes, the Abdali or Durrani tribes, which live in the area around Kandahar and Herat, in the south and west respectively, and the Ghilzai, who live in the Nangarhar–Paktia region. The Ghilzai, along with the eastern tribes living in Pakistan who speak a different dialect, remain Pashtuns. Thus, when the British established the modern boundary of Afghanistan and India along the Durand Line in 1893, they artificially separated ethnic Afghans on both sides of the frontier. The Durranis have provided the kings and oligarchy of the country since the mid-18th century, although during the communist era (1973–92) national leaders were always drawn from the Ghilzai confederacy.

The language spoken by Pashtuns is related to Persian (Farsi), consists of a complex system of grammar, with much borrowing from Arabic and Persian, and is written in an alphabet modified from Arabic. Many Pashtuns learn Dari as well, although Pashto has formed the national language since 1964. Nearly all Pashtuns are Sunni Muslims, with a small number of Shi'a among the eastern tribes. Tribal or inter-clan interaction is based on a tribal legal system known as Pashtunwali and much tribal business is achieved through the tribal assembly or *Jirga*.

ETHNO-LINGUISTIC GROUPS IN AND AROUND AFGHANISTAN

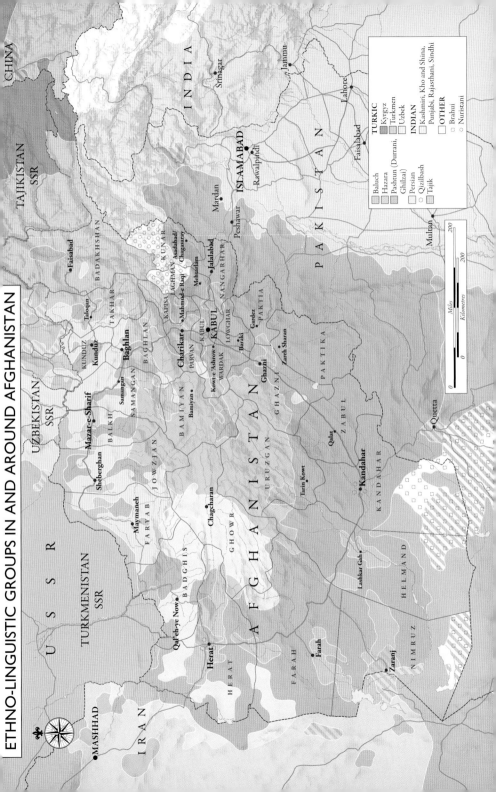

TURKIC		INDIAN
Kyrgyz		Kashmiri, Kho and Shina,
Turkmen		Punjabi, Rajasthani, Sindhi
Uzbek		**OTHER**
		Brahui
		Nuristani

Baluch
Hazara
Pashtun (Durrani, Ghilzai)
Persian
Qizilbash
Tajik

Tajiks, who live in the northern, north-eastern, and western parts of Afghanistan, tend to speak Dari or Afghan Persian, languages familiar to the Farsiwan who are nevertheless unrelated ethnically, as are the Qizilbash and the Hazara of the central region of the country. All are related linguistically, though the Tajiks and Farsiwan are Sunni Muslims like most Pashtuns, whereas the Qizilbash and the Hazara profess Shi'a Islam in the style of the Iranians. The Tajiks' loyalty rests with village and family, but unlike the Pashtuns, who place strong emphasis on genealogy and tribal history, they can integrate more successfully amongst their own communities transplanted elsewhere in the country. Historically they have been denied positions of leadership in politics or the military.

The Hazaras, who live in the central part of Afghanistan, constitute less than 10 per cent of the population, and operate a social structure in which various individuals exercise significant authority, such as the headman, chief, or *malik* (known locally as a *mir*). His position of reverence derives from his status as a landowner and from a hereditary status purportedly descending from the line of the Prophet Muhammad. They are racially akin to the Mongols, whose physical features set them readily apart from other ethnic groups and have led to discrimination over the centuries, particularly by the Pashtuns, who often used them as servants and slaves. The Hazaras' adherence to the Shi'a sect has furthered the degree of discrimination directed against them, leaving them somewhat on the fringes of society, a condition exacerbated by their physical isolation in the Hazarajat, which suffered considerably less from Soviet occupation and the Afghan civil war than most other areas.

Afghanistan also contains ethnic Turkic-speaking groups living in the north, including about a million Uzbeks, 200,000 Turkmens, and about 15,000 Kazakhs, with co-ethnic peoples who at the time of the war lived just over the border in Soviet Central Asia, and of course continue to do so in the now-independent republics.

Most engage in agriculture or raise animals and speak their own language, although many are bilingual in Dari, which serves as the inter-ethnic language in the north. Generally speaking, the Uzbeks largely do not have strong tribal affiliations, whereas the Turkmens are closely tied to their own. Other ethnic groups, which make up the dozen or more smaller ethnicities in Afghanistan, speak between them more than 20 languages and dialects, though they are largely illiterate, and live almost entirely rural and for the most part segregated lives owing to geographical isolation.

Although 85 percent of Afghans lived in the countryside in 1979, falling to 79 per cent a decade later, and to 74 per cent in 2021, their patterns of life vary. Again, in addition to the binding nature of Islam, major unifying elements include close family relationships, patterns of living which stretch back dozens of generations, living close to and depending upon the land for practically all their needs, and a close observance to a faith in a largely unchanging life for the community as a whole. The typical Afghan adheres to a tradition of loyalty first to family, then to village, then to tribe, and finally to

A farmer in Wardak province. Conservative rural dwellers rejected the government's progressive social and political reforms as inimical to Afghan traditions and culture and to Islam. (Photo by José Nicolas/Corbis via Getty Images)

ethnic group. This accounts for the poor development of patriotism, the long-standing problem of creating a national identity, and the difficulties associated with central government trying to spread its authority across a sprawling, mountainous conglomeration of diverse peoples speaking different languages and practising different customs. But if loyalty may be identified as a central guiding tenet of rural Afghan life, so too must bravery. In 1985 Arthur Bonner succinctly observed that:

> Bravery is central to the Afghans. Being brave, or just seeming brave, shapes their attitudes toward life and the people around them. A large part of bravery in Afghan eyes is being able to bear pain and suffering. Honor is also important, and honor to the Afghans means not taking second place to anyone. They don't like to be pushed around. It offends their honor and makes them want to get even. Revenge is another part of what it means to be a man in Afghanistan. The proof of these generalities is that Afghanistan, a poor and mountainous nation, with no technology and only light arms has literally stopped the Soviet Army dead in its tracks. (Bonner 1987: 1)

Accommodation in rural areas varies according to region, but before outlining its features it is germane to note that nationwide, one in nine houses in the countryside was believed uninhabitable in 1993, while in Nangarhar province, in the east, only 60 per cent were habitable. Of the approximately 15,000 villages in Afghanistan at the outset of the war, approximately 13 per cent of those in the southeast would suffer from problems of mines in agricultural areas, in irrigation systems, near houses, and along roads. Still, while wide-scale Soviet bombing depleted the countryside of its population, it did not fundamentally alter the basic structure of life for those who remained. Rural Pashtuns live in *qalas*, which are fortified, fired or sun-dried brick dwellings housing whole extended families and covered with curved roofs topped with flat ones. These structures feature rooms facing inwards towards a courtyard, with the rooms to the rear abutting the compound wall that can rise to 10ft or higher. The whole family lives within the safety of this compound, through whose single entrance all pass until the gate is bolted at night. While nuclear families occupy rooms exclusive to themselves, sleeping and keeping their personal possessions, the kitchen and toilet areas, as well as food storage areas and accommodation for guests, are shared by the extended family. Rural life depends heavily upon well-defined, gender-specific roles, with men responsible for building and maintaining accommodation, buying and selling goods and services, managing flocks of sheep and goats, and planting, ploughing, maintaining the irrigation system, and any other work which demands their presence in public. Women care for children, assist in harvesting the crops, pursue crafts like quilt-making, and manage the family's domestic animals. Most roles are also defined by the age of the individual, as more advanced age necessarily commands respect. In such a cohesive, traditional community as a large *qala*, one may find many dozens of people of several generations living and working together.

A group of *qalas* typically figure within or near a village, with irrigated fields either amidst them or nearby. Services, including shops, roads, and public buildings in the vicinity, are basic. Many *qalas* contain a small mosque and sometimes a bathhouse within the compound, while others, such as those near the cities of Kandahar and Herat, often consist of more substantial structures of vaulted one-storey buildings constructed from sun-dried bricks. A group of such structures is sometimes found connected, with a single compound wall protecting everyone, which may include up to three generations of a family. Compounds normally contain a small stable for chickens and cows or other domestic animals, while storage areas hold supplies of food and fuel for a whole year. A well within the compound provides clean water, but rural dwellers sometimes make use of streams or the irrigation system. To keep warm in the winter, rural Afghans burn charcoal in small braziers, which form a central point around which people sit, propping themselves up against the walls with cushions and bedding behind and a quilt covering the lower body. Sometimes in the centre of the room a brazier sits in a shallow depression dug into the ground, with a low table above covered by a quilt and tablecloth, so placed to function as a place for eating and socializing.

Rural Afghans tend to dress in a manner specifically intended to identify their ethnic group. Men often wear distinctive turbans or turban caps, with the method of tying the cloth (*lungi* or *dastar*) of the former identifying the group to which a man belongs. The turban cap (*kolah*) reflects a particular ethnic group by its specific embroidery. Most men also wear a loose-fitting, long-tailed cotton shirt that slips over the head and hangs to the knees or even lower, fastened by buttons on one shoulder. Baggy trousers with a drawstring waist, out of which the shirttail usually remains untucked, together with a sleeveless, often distinctively embroidered waistcoat (*waskat*) or vest over the shirt, nearly complete this fairly standard outfit worn throughout the countryside. But notwithstanding variation according to region, one garment finds universal use, as Bonner noted in 1985:

> A thin blanket is an integral part of the Afghan costume and has many uses. Generally a man folds it during the day and carries it on one shoulder. When the air is chilly, he wraps the blanket around his shoulders. If it is extra cold, he drapes it over his head to keep his ears warm. Under a hot sun he folds it into a thick pad and places it on top of his head to keep it cool. He spreads it on the ground as a clean area for prayers. He drapes it over his back like a curtain when he goes into an open field to relieve himself. If a man has a number of things to carry, he wraps them in the blanket and knots the ends in front of his chest so that it becomes a sort of pack. If he sits on the ground he folds the blanket under him as a cushion and also to keep his trousers from getting dirty. But its main use is to keep him warm. (Bonner 1987: 14)

Women universally wear the shawl (or *chadar*), which is multi-functional, protecting her from dirt while allowing

her to preserve a degree of modesty, since she can partly cover her face from a passing stranger by gripping a corner with her teeth. She can also wrap a baby and feed it in privacy by using one end of her *chadar*, and by tying a corner of it she may transport small items. Rural women usually wear a white or coloured cotton shirt, baggy trousers, or an ankle-length skirt, with styles varying greatly according to region and climate. Footwear varies greatly, too, from open-toed and open-heeled leather or straw sandals to various types of boots, particularly in the colder north, where knitted, knee-length, thick wool stockings are worn inside boots during winter.

Numerous books devote themselves to Afghan history, geography, culture, and religion, and nothing more than a thumbnail sketch of rural life may be outlined here. However, in delving further into these subjects the profound obstacles to change encountered by those politicians, bureaucrats, and reformers who between 1978 and 1992 sought to tamper with the fundamentally traditional, religiously conservative nature of rural Afghanistan emerge in stark relief.

Government militiamen in the background guarding a village in Paghman province, where fighting took place against the Mujahideen in January 1987. (Photo by DERRICK CEYRAC/AFP via Getty Images)

HOW THE WAR ENDED
UN diplomacy and Soviet withdrawal

Over time neither overwhelming military force nor the internal reforms undertaken by the Soviets and their Afghan protégés could hope to crush the insurgency. While some Afghans, particularly those in the cities and above all the educated classes, collaborated with the Soviets, DRA forces stood distinctively subordinate to their counterparts. In that role, given their consistently poor operational record, morale necessarily suffered and declined. Neither Soviet nor Afghan leaders could offer a political solution to continued resistance, and with an impasse in the field stretching far longer than ever anticipated, stirrings in Moscow began to encourage withdrawal, not least because the Mujahideen demonstrated no inclination to negotiate under circumstances where compromise offered them nothing.

Accordingly, Moscow began to appreciate in 1985 that the war had become unwinnable. Chernenko and Andropov, both of whom succeeded Brezhnev as party secretary for brief periods (November 1982–February 1984 and February 1984–March 1985, respectively), suffered from ill health during their entire periods in office, during which they failed to exercise the energy and leadership required to keep the insurgency under control, much less destroy it. This obliged the Central Committee to appoint a younger man to finish the job. Coming to power on 10 March 1985, Mikhail Gorbachev inherited an intractable war, as the chief of the Soviet General Staff, Marshal Sergei Akhromeyev (1923–91), explained:

> In the past seven years Soviet soldiers have had their boots on the ground in every square kilometre of the country. But as soon as they left, the enemy returned and restored everything the way it was before. We have lost this war. The majority of the Afghan people support the counter-revolution. We have lost the peasantry, who have got nothing from the revolution. 80% of the country is in the hands of the counter-revolution. And the position of the peasants there is better than it is on the territory controlled by the government. (Quoted in Johnson 2011: 241)

Gorbachev represented a fresh start in Soviet foreign policy as well as in domestic politics. He was a leader

Some Soviet personnel of reasonably good quality served in Afghanistan, but the corrupt conscription system sometimes dispatched men because they failed to pay bribes. (Photo by Robert Nickelsberg/Getty Images)

whose policy of *glasnost* (openness) had from the beginning of his time in office already tolerated internal – and even public – criticism of the war, and who recognized the strategic errors committed by his country. His desire to extricate troops from Afghanistan centred on three key motives. First and foremost, the failing prospects of the war rendered further operations pointless. Second, withdrawal would provide a mechanism by which to improve the Soviet Union's relations with the West, particularly with the United States at a time when the issue of nuclear disarmament remained high on both countries' agendas. Indeed, even if the Carter administration's (1977–81) boycott of the 1980 Moscow Olympics and the embargo of American grain shipments to the Soviet Union had constituted nothing more than irritation, Carter's and the subsequent Reagan administration's (1981–89) refusal to continue talks to try to ratify the proposed SALT II restrictions on nuclear weapons stood indefinitely postponed as a result of the invasion, and Gorbachev could countenance this no longer. Third, with domestic discontent partly assuaged by the troops' return and military expenditure reduced, he could concentrate on the social, economic, and political reforms urgently needed within the USSR.

The origins of the decision to withdraw require brief examination. Anatoly Dobrynin (1919–2010), the Soviet ambassador to the United States between 1962 and 1986, claimed that at a Politburo meeting of 17 October 1985 Gorbachev declared, 'It's time to leave', to which the other members raised no objection. They fixed no date for final withdrawal, but the die had been cast. Debate continues about the degree to which this meeting represented the first concrete decision to bring an end to the war, but any doubts may be cast aside by the decisive results of the Politburo meeting held on 13 November 1986, in which Akhromeyev made a devastatingly prescient and unchallengeable assertion: 'We have lost the battle for the Afghan people'. Accordingly, Gorbachev proposed that the Soviet Union should withdraw its forces over a two-year period, with half removed in 1987 and the rest to leave the following year, a recommendation to which the other members gave their assent. Here stood the idea in principle; now Gorbachev needed the mechanism by which to implement it.

To lay the groundwork for troop withdrawal, Soviet authorities sought to expand DRA forces to enable them to take a more active combat role. However, this did not achieve the desired effect, since government military personnel continued to perform unreliably against their compatriots in the resistance, leaving Soviet troops to continue to bear the greatest burden in combat. This compounded anxiety over the likelihood of a smooth transition of security affairs to the Kabul regime, already looking grim in light of Najibullah's continuing failure successfully to implement his programme of reforms. Gennady Bocharov was probably not alone in expressing anxiety about the competence of the Soviet advisors serving in Kabul. While he acknowledged that some Central Asian specialists served in Afghanistan, most were merely city and regional party secretaries:

> They knew absolutely nothing about the east. Their conception of Afghanistan was hazy, to say the least … but the standard party advisers dealt with practical matters. They were not interested in consultations. As for those who were charged with devising strategy and tactics – they frankly ignored the opinions of any specialist …
>
> The trouble with the advisers was not just that they didn't know Afghanistan. They did not know something even more important: how to run things in their own backyard, let alone a foreign country. (Bocharov 1990: 61)

In short, it became clear that Moscow would eventually have to withdraw from Afghanistan in as honourable a fashion as possible and thus leave Najibullah to his own devices, albeit heavily subsidized with food, weapons and materiel.

The United Nations stood as the obvious intermediary between the belligerents. Gorbachev depended on it to

Mohammad Najibullah, who before becoming president of the DRA in May 1986 headed the infamous KhAD, or secret police. (Photo by Patrick ROBERT/Sygma via Getty Images)

achieve this role, with the Afghan government effectively representing Soviet interests and Pakistan acting on behalf of the Mujahideen, since Islamabad unofficially supported the resistance, while the United States by extension supported the same through Pakistan. As such, negotiations conducted by the United Nations, if successful, stood to benefit the interests of all the principal parties to the conflict, belligerents and non-belligerents alike. Having said this, accords brokered by the UN necessarily set some limitations on its freedom of action in light of the Soviet Union's position as a permanent member of the Security Council. That fact had protected the aggressor in 1979, since the Soviet Union could veto the UN's original condemnation of its invasion. Now, nearly a decade later, for the sake of extricating themselves from an unwinnable war, the Soviets were happily prepared to regard the UN as a third party in the process of 'conflict resolution' by accepting its 'good offices' and the shuttle diplomacy it could offer. Specifically, the Secretary General, by the authority of the UN, could engage in negotiations unilaterally, supported by the UN Secretariat.

The Geneva Peace Accords, concluded in March 1988, enabled the Soviets to begin the process of withdrawing their troops from Afghanistan. (Photo by THIERRY ORBAN/Sygma via Getty Images)

The Geneva Accords were signed on 14 April 1988, by which the Soviets agreed to remove their forces from Afghanistan. Other essential elements established for Afghanistan and Pakistan a policy of mutual non-interference and non-intervention with respect to sovereignty, economic stability, and territorial integrity. According to one section of Article II, neither side could train, equip, finance, or recruit mercenaries, whatever

their origin, for the purpose of engaging in hostile activity in either party's territory, including the maintenance of bases for purposes of supporting outside forces. As such, the DRA was to be left to its own devices with respect to subduing its own domestic insurgency and could not accept foreign intervention, though this did not preclude money and weapons.

For the various parties concerned, this represented a reasonable outcome, notwithstanding the fact that no delegates directly represented the Mujahideen. Attempting to negotiate with the disparate groups that comprised the resistance – represented by seven different political parties, all based in Pakistan – would probably have been futile, as any accord would inevitably have required separate agreements with rival groups, a course almost certain to prolong the conflict and lead to fighting between factions within the Mujahideen competing for power in a post-communist Afghanistan. But while the settlement enabled the Soviets to claim that they had finally accorded with international calls for their withdrawal, they obviously could not ensure a peaceful outcome between their surrogates in Kabul and the resistance. Thus, the Geneva Accords merely brought to a close one dimension of the Afghan civil war. If anything, every prospect still existed for that bitter struggle to continue in the wake of Soviet withdrawal, a struggle that, it is important to recall, had begun in 1978 before the Soviet invasion (though some may argue the insurgency properly dated from Daoud's accession to power in 1973).

The withdrawal signalled the international isolation of Najibullah's regime, formalized when diplomats from key Western nations closed their embassies in Kabul. West Germany began the process on 21 January 1989, followed on the 27th by France, Britain, Japan, and Italy. The United States withdrew its diplomatic staff three days later, only reopening its embassy in December 2001 when its troops retook Kabul from the Taliban in the wake of the 9/11 attacks. Meanwhile, the passing of Soviet troops back over the border went largely unchallenged

Demonstration of the Communist People's Democratic Party of Afghanistan (PDPA) in Kabul during the period of Soviet troop withdrawal. (Photo by Patrick ROBERT/ Sygma via Getty Images)

by the resistance, though the Soviets themselves, anxious to prevent attacks on their forces as they withdrew, staged a campaign of terror, largely with concentrated artillery fire, against villages along their route towards the frontier so as to intimidate the Mujahideen into restraint. Thousands streamed away from their villages as vast Soviet columns trundled through the smoke of the devastation left in their wake. Finally, on 15 February, General Boris Gromov, commander of the 40th Army and the last Soviet soldier to leave the country, crossed the bridge at Termez, so putting an end to a tragic adventure fraught with human folly and misguided ambition.

In the immediate wake of the Soviets' departure the Mujahideen largely ceased their operations, preserving and expanding their resources and manpower for the day when they would oppose other factions vying for sole control of government machinery in Kabul. Civil war was encouraged by the fact that rival groups expected some influence on the war's outcome in compensation for the effort expended since its beginning. Indeed, internecine fighting was bound to continue until a sole victor emerged. Any power-sharing was unlikely, for competing factions possessed no mechanism for building trust between rivals, and no agreement existed to divide responsibility for the rebuilding of the country's devastated infrastructure, for control over the military and security forces, or for the distribution of political power, amongst many other issues. As a natural consequence of these and many other factors, the fighting continued for another three years, mostly against the government, but with some clashes between insurgent groups. During this period the Soviets continued to fund Najibullah's government, leaving in its hands an enormous stockpile of weapons and ammunition that enabled the president to maintain his increasingly tenuous grip on power. But that is to anticipate events: in the post-withdrawal period the Soviet Union established the greatest air-bridge since the Berlin Blockade of 1948, furnishing aid to the DRA estimated at a staggering $300 million a month, with one report indicating that weapons alone delivered

OPPOSITE
Mujahideen outside their camp in Charikar, near Kabul, celebrate the end of the Najibullah regime in April 1992. (Photo by RAVI RAVEENDRAN/AFP via Getty Images)

in the six months after February 1989 carried a value of $1.4 billion.

However, matters continued to deteriorate for the Afghan regime, a fact underscored by the attempted coup staged by General Shahnawaz Tanai (1950–2022) in April 1990, after which Najibullah understandably

took an increasingly dim view of the loyalty of his security forces, which declined in strength from as many as 400,000 (including army, paramilitary police, and KhAD) in 1989 to 160,000 in 1991. His subsequent actions betrayed a man narrowly clinging to power. After his desperate appeals to rural leaders for stability and co-operation were rejected, he turned to raising sizeable militias to achieve the objectives that his unreliable regular forces could not. In Herat, a hotbed of resistance, government militia increased from about 14,000 in 1986 to 70,000 in 1991, largely through attractive offers of arms and money to Mujahideen leaders prepared to defect with their fighters to the government now that the Soviet threat had passed, and Kabul could supply their needs. A fifth of former Mujahideen groups shifted to the government side and recast themselves as loyalist militia, while a further 40 per cent accepted offers of a ceasefire. The rest remained irreconcilable. Ironically, these new units proved to be the president's undoing, for they grew so large – 170,000 in 1991, accounting for over 50 per cent of government forces – as to become practically self-governing in their own areas of operation, and when with the collapse of the Soviet Union Moscow immediately ceased funding the DRA, the various militias refused to obey orders from Najibullah's now transparently tottering regime. In many cases these rogue forces established themselves as independent units under the more powerful militia commanders, who fashioned themselves into warlords. Some of these controlled extensive areas almost as fiefdoms, collecting taxes and administering their own laws, and operating in an increasingly chaotic and unstable state. Less powerful militia groups mimicked this practice, either vying for control over smaller areas theoretically under government authority or over other militia groups. In so doing they inaugurated a new period of the existing civil war that followed the fall of Najibullah's regime in April 1992, and which continued even after the Taliban seized Kabul in 1996, by which time the loss in human life may even have exceeded that of the period of Soviet occupation.

CONCLUSION AND CONSEQUENCES

Impact on the USSR

Statistics connected with the Soviets' role in the war make for depressing reading. Total forces deployed over the whole course of the conflict amounted to approximately 642,000 personnel. Of these, approximately 545,000 served in the regular forces, while another 90,000 came from armed KGB units. Perhaps 5,000 belonged to the MVD (*Ministerstvo Vnutrennikh Del* or Ministry of Internal Affairs). Statistics for the dead and missing vary according to the source consulted, but range between 13,000 and 15,000 personnel, 35,000 to 37,000 wounded, and about 300 missing in action. Perhaps 40,000 Afghan government forces were killed or wounded, and DRA troop desertions ranged between 50,000 and 60,000 personnel. A total of 10,751 Soviet soldiers became invalids, many as amputees. Yet these already substantial figures must be seen in light of the 469,685 sick and wounded – or over 70 per cent of the total force – discharged and repatriated. Statistics for those stricken with disease tell an even more revealing story: a staggering 415,932 cases, of whom 115,308 men suffered from infectious hepatitis and 31,080 from typhoid fever. The sheer scale of sickness reveals the dreadful state of hygiene prevalent within the Soviet forces and their appalling conditions in the field.

The pressure on Soviet hospitals – particularly with respect to long-term illness and the disabled – can only be reckoned to have been enormous, with correspondingly

Mujahideen with one of 30 destroyed Antonov-32 Soviet cargo and troop transports on the runway of a Kabul airbase after a 16-day battle in 1992. (Photo by Robert Nickelsberg/Getty Images)

serious social implications for society as a whole. In sharp contrast to their fathers who had defended the country against the German menace during World War

II, soldiers returning from Afghanistan not only received no hero's welcome but often felt shunned by a public detached from, if not actually hostile to, the war. The loss in materiel and equipment also helps place in perspective the scale of the conflict and offers a sharp lesson to those who would slavishly rely on technology alone as some sort of magical panacea for all problems operational: 118 jets, 333 helicopters, 147 tanks, 1,314 armoured personnel carriers, 433 artillery pieces and mortars, 1,138 radio sets and CP vehicles, 510 engineering vehicles, and 11,369 trucks.

Even before the troops returned, the impact of the war at home had become palpable. The Soviet military experience in Afghanistan amounted to a slow, attritional effort, which not only demonstrated the declining combat effectiveness of the USSR's armed forces, but revealed stark, irreparable cracks developing within the Soviet political infrastructure. Society itself underwent change owing to the rotation in and out of Afghanistan of conscripted troops, whose disappointments and stories of hardship and frustration permeated Soviet society, undermining morale and sowing seeds of doubt in respect to both the war effort and also the people's confidence in the country's political and economic system as a whole. Thus, problems experienced in Afghanistan manifested themselves back home, and one might contend that internal disintegration affected Soviet troops' morale in theatre. The two, in any event, proved mutually corrosive, albeit within a process that must be seen as gradual, like that of the growing body count of the war.

While only a small percentage of the population served in the war or was touched by it as a consequence of the loss of a son, brother, or husband, the Soviet experience in Afghanistan created a large body of disaffected veterans of the conflict. Known as the *afgantsy*, these veterans' disillusionment at home manifested itself over a range of emotions, from unexpressed derision of Moscow to outright criticism of the Soviet system in general. Such veterans did not organize themselves into any form of political movement or lobby, but in light of Gorbachev's growing liberalization of Soviet society as a consequence of his policies of *glasnost* ('openness') and *perestroika* (literally 're-structuring', involving wholesale changes to the Soviet state), the attitudes of Afghan veterans nevertheless played some part in influencing public opinion and contributing to the general atmosphere of disgruntled citizens now prepared to question decisions made at all levels of government, including the Kremlin. In short, the war became a metaphor for systemic problems within Soviet society, and thus accelerated the rate of social and political change under way since Gorbachev had come to power in the spring of 1985. The cost of the war exacerbated such problems, for expenditure ran into the billions and placed an enormous strain on the Soviet economy, which continued with the flow of supplies to Najibullah's regime after the troops returned home.

Criticism of communist rule, or at least its existing form, also developed from within, for the war led to a loss of faith in the party leadership amongst the middle and upper echelons of the Communist Party

Soviet veterans of the war in Afghanistan pay homage to fallen comrades at a ceremony in Moscow in June 1988. (DOMINIQUE FAGET/AFP via Getty Images)

itself. Whereas before and during the Brezhnev era the party elite tended to operate on the basis of intra-party consultation, this practice had rapidly declined during the years of intervention in Afghanistan, prompting those of a reformist disposition to use the failing military effort as a means to push through their agendas and thus speed the process of change. Many analysts point to the declining Soviet economy, the inability of the state to continue to bear the burden of subsidizing communist allies around the world, Afghanistan included, and the impossibility of trying to match the United States in the nuclear arms race as the prime movers in the collapse of the Soviet Union.

In the end the Soviets had intervened on the basis of supporting a notionally communist state; in reality, from 1978 the succession of Afghan regimes only attracted widespread domestic condemnation followed by open hostility and civil war. The fact of Soviet withdrawal in 1989 – with little to show for it but a deeply unpopular satellite government condemned to hold down an insurgency that even the Soviets had failed to contain, much less defeat – went far in eroding the long-held Soviet doctrine that socialism represented a positive and irreversible movement for the political, social, and economic good of peoples across the globe.

Why the Soviets lost

The Soviets and their DRA ally enjoyed an overwhelming advantage in firepower both on the ground and in the air, as well as in terms of transport, communications, and technology. Together they could control the infrastructure of the cities, prevail in nearly every engagement with the Mujahideen, pacify large rural areas, and maintain logistic hubs and supply routes with levels of security sufficient to conduct operations across wide areas of the country. All this beggars the question as to how they could possibly fail, to which the answers are numerous and varied in nature, but in aggregate account for a defeat by no means inevitable.

The Soviets hamstrung themselves through a complete lack of preparation for a long struggle of major proportions. By invading Afghanistan in December 1979, they intended to execute a mere *coup d'état*, overthrowing a weak and unpopular regime, albeit one sympathetic to Marxist principles and friendly to the USSR. Against minimal opposition, the Soviets accordingly seized control of the apparatus of government and the country's infrastructure; and yet the occupiers failed to achieve the most critical objective of all – political stability by securing the confidence of the people in their own government – as evidenced by the string of puppet administrations the invaders progressively installed to replace the one they had ousted. From the outset, and until the time they departed nine years hence, the Soviets found that what they euphemistically termed 'assistance' to their beleaguered fellow communist state, the great majority of Afghans (not to mention most of the world beyond Moscow's sphere) transparently recognized it for what it was – forcible occupation – a reality which did far more than simply attract the ire of ordinary Afghans; it alienated all but certain elements of urban dwellers from their own government. The Soviets could not have foreseen that what in their minds ought to have comprised a simple, straightforward incursion of very limited duration, would in fact escalate into years of frustrating struggle akin to the American experience in Vietnam. While hubris may explain the Soviets' initial miscalculation, it took years for them to recognize the hopelessness of the endeavour, since by their reckoning the natural order of military logic dictated that any contest pitting their conventional forces against an insurgency – particularly one plagued by disunity, almost entirely reliant on light arms, and hampered by numerical inferiority at the tactical level at the very least – ought ultimately to turn in the Soviets' favour.

There is no question that the Soviet war effort suffered from poor or virtually non-existent political direction. The series of either ineffective political masters in Moscow or the regularity with which they sickened and died off during the 1980s contributed in no small way towards Soviet failure. Brezhnev, not healthy at the time of the invasion, became incapacitated the following year and did not succumb to his illness until November 1982, leaving all decisions to committees exercising collective leadership. His successor, Yuri Andropov, lasted less than two years, and upon his death in February 1984, Konstantin Chernenko survived for little more than a year until his own demise. During this whole period the conflict was allowed to carry on with little in the way of decision-making over substantial issues concerning the conduct of operations or the overall purpose of the war. When at last Gorbachev took the helm in March 1985 and found that the war could not be brought to a conclusion within a year – in fact Soviet casualties rose to record levels during that period – he sought a means to withdraw in a dignified fashion, which as we have seen the United Nations provided.

Quite apart from its poor and ever-changing political direction, the Soviet Union could not bear the spiralling cost of the war. While it is difficult to establish the financial burden with any degree of certainty, a CIA intelligence assessment from 1987 estimated the average expenditure on military assistance from 1980 to 1986 at approximately $7 billion *per year*. Only approximate figures can be provided for Soviet economic – that is, non-lethal – aid to the Afghan government, but this ranged from between $200 million and $350 million annually, although a sizeable proportion funded the DRA's war effort. Having said this, the government in Kabul itself bore a substantial part of the financial burden of the war, with ever-increasing expenditure on defence, estimated at $180 to $290 million annually from 1980 to 1988. As a percentage of the national budget, military spending rose to approximately 30 per cent by 1980–82, but more than doubled in the years 1983 to 1988, inclusive – quite simply, colossal and unsustainable costs.

Soviet counterinsurgency strategy suffered from a number of other weaknesses. Just as the Americans in Vietnam could not effectively disrupt the many supply

routes running between North and South Vietnam via Laos and Cambodia – chiefly by means of the Ho Chi Minh Trail – the Soviets failed to control the 2,640km (1,640 mile) long, porous border separating Afghanistan and Pakistan to the east, and that with Iran, measuring 936km (582 miles) to the west. Insurgent communication networks remained largely intact, as well. Moscow's inability both to interdict the massive influx of foreign aid to the Mujahideen and to prevent the insurgents' regular, often unhindered, access to safe havens in ostensibly neutral countries, greatly hampered the Soviet military effort. Compounding these intractable problems, the Kremlin failed to make a more concerted effort to drive a wedge between the disparate rebel groups, exploiting their differences, be they political, tribal, ethnic, ideological, or religious.

The almost total absence of a 'hearts and minds' campaign undoubtedly contributed to Soviet failure, leaving them to focus almost entirely on search-and-destroy operations, much like the policy of the Rhodesian government during the Bush War of 1965–80, in which a short-sighted and misdirected emphasis on military operations in preference to political initiatives led to a remarkable string of impressive tactical successes in the field, yet utterly failed at the strategic level as a consequence of the Smith regime's refusal to grant political concessions to the black majority or to provide practical aid to rural dwellers in a bid somehow to preserve white minority rule. What little effort the Soviets made on the hearts and minds front – hindered as they were by their failure adequately to understand Afghanistan's culture, traditions, religious sensibilities, and numerous languages – they squandered through the brutal methods which came to exemplify their style of pacification.

In the event, the Soviets had, like their adversaries, to adapt and innovate, but did so far less effectively. The experience of initial contact with the Mujahideen revealed the poor quality of 40th Army's infantry training and the questionable utility of many of the weapons and weapon systems deployed in an insurgency for the character and scale of which the Soviets were unprepared. It took five years before Soviet troops and Afghan government forces developed new tactics and reorganized their units to meet the challenge of asymmetric warfare. Small, much more mobile units, working in tandem with helicopter assault assets, together with large-scale bombing, had by 1985 enhanced Soviet capabilities to such an extent as to threaten the sustainability of insurgent opposition. But such improvements in the Soviets' fortunes had materialized too late, and in the end the war constituted a strategic blunder, for there existed no geo-strategic rationale for the involvement of the USSR in Afghan affairs given the resources required.

With respect to resources, it is clear the Soviets failed to deploy sufficient numbers of personnel, particularly forces actually willing and able to get to grips with the enemy, as opposed to those in support and administrative roles, important though those roles are. Instead of an average of approximately 120,000 troops on the ground, they probably required three or four times as many. Parallels with the 1960s are imperfect here, since in Vietnam the United States faced conventional as well as guerrilla forces; but it is worth noting that in the spring of 1968, at the height of their troop levels in South Vietnam – a country about a quarter the size of Afghanistan – Americans forces numbered 536,000, with the personnel fielded by the Saigon government well exceeding this figure, at approximately 800,000, plus more than 60,000 others, mostly South Koreans and Australians. Yet even these impressive numbers failed to meet the military challenge, even when one throws into the calculus the presence of North Vietnamese regulars to confront on top of the Viet Cong. This begs the question as to what chance of success the Soviets had when they fielded but a fraction of such numbers.

Still, war cannot be reduced simply to a numbers game, for there remain those intangible, unquantifiable, though nonetheless critically important factors which also influence success and failure, such as will, resilience, and moral commitment. In all of these, as well as in crude numerical strength, the Soviets and their Afghan allies stood woefully deficient. In summary, the war demonstrated that even a superpower with access to the most sophisticated weaponry cannot regard victory over irregular forces as a foregone conclusion, a fact reconfirmed by the outcome of the NATO campaign from 2001 to 2014.

Impact on Afghanistan

Statistics vary on the unnatural, war-related Afghan deaths that occurred during the Soviet occupation, but range from between 900,000 to 1.3 million people. The Mujahideen lost between 140,000 and 200,000 full-time fighters killed or wounded, and another 40,000 to 90,000 supporting civilians or part-time fighters killed or wounded. Yet this already staggering scale of combined military and civilian fatalities must not obscure the record of suffering caused to ordinary villagers through injury and disability. An estimated 1.5 million Afghan civilians became physically disabled as a result of the war. In addition, the psychological trauma caused by the conflict was both unquantifiable and virtually untreatable in the 1980s in a country bereft of facilities or suitable personnel, not to mention a prevailing culture that does not recognize depression properly and stigmatizes those who fail to conceal the trauma associated with that condition. The Soviets also sowed and left behind millions of mines, which continue to kill and maim. These bare facts speak volumes for the colossal scale of this tragedy.

Vast numbers of Afghans became displaced as a result of the war, with over 6 million refugees – 2.9 million in Pakistan, 1.9 million in Iran, and 1.2 million internally displaced – representing at least a third of the pre-war population living under miserable conditions beyond Afghanistan's borders in Iran and Pakistan by the early 1990s. Most benefited to some extent from the efforts of both the Pakistani and Iranian authorities to provide aid to this massive influx of humanity, but in the end the absence of these refugees from their villages left large numbers of people without skills otherwise acquired and practised in farming and cottage-industry activity. Quite apart from those already possessing some skills, young people found themselves denied the ability to learn a trade, engage in agriculture, or to manage and herd livestock. To this huge number of external refugees must be added those internally displaced. The population of Kabul grew considerably as rural dwellers flocked to the capital in search of protection from air attack in the countryside. Women and children suffered particularly badly, since while their menfolk were away serving in government units or as resistance fighters, they were left to manage for themselves in the devastation caused by aerial mines and high explosives scattered over and around mud-brick homes and compounds whose simple structures offered no protection from such ordnance. Quite apart from the social isolation which arose, women suffered from the loss of the wages their husbands normally brought home

The Soviets are estimated to have laid between 10 million and 16 million mines during the war, many as booby traps or outside plotted minefields. (Photo by Peter Turnley/Corbis/VCG via Getty Images)

to feed families in a society where the long-term absence or death of a father and/or his sons could produce serious disruption to family life, financially as well as socially.

Young Afghan orphaned refugees who fled the area of Kabul gather in the Bajaur refugee camp in Pakistan, March 1980. (Photo by AFP via Getty Images)

Apart from the damage inflicted on the population, the war saw severe disruption to the Afghan economy, largely through the physical effects of bombing and

artillery fire. The Soviets sought out targets representing important elements of the country's infrastructure, while the absence of regular maintenance left other elements useless after years of neglect, owing to lack of parts or the absence of trained personnel to maintain machinery. As discussed, mud-brick housing offered no protection against high explosives, whether delivered on the ground or from the air, with the result that by the early 1990s, 60 per cent of schools did not possess a physical structure. The country already lacked a railway system and boasted little more than a rudimentary road network, apart from the massive ring road that the Americans had built long before the war. What remained deteriorated during the 1980s, in turn adversely affecting trade and thus the economy as a whole, quite apart from rendering refugees' journeys all the more arduous. Moreover, general destruction, attributable to both sides, accounted for the loss of more than 1,800 schools, 31 hospitals, 11 health centres, and 14,000km (8,700 miles) of telephone cable.

The war also severely disrupted agriculture, the mainstay of the country's economy, to a great extent. While prior to the coup in 1978 Afghanistan unquestionably constituted a poor country, it did not qualify as one suffering from hunger. By 1987, however, this had changed, since agricultural output had sharply declined to only a third of 1978 figures as a result of the loss of land suitable for cultivation, a decline by a half of land once available for cultivation but now unusable owing, for instance, to the wide-scale deaths of draught oxen. The bombardment of hundreds of villages and wide areas of cultivated land in order to force the population off the land and into the cities – or in any event away from areas considered vital to the Soviets – accounted for much of this deliberately inflicted damage.

Afghanistan also suffered a severe decline in its balance of payments owing to a sharp rise in imports and a contrasting fall in exports. The country's trade deficit rose in 1980 from $69 million – representing 9.8 per cent of exports – to $649 million or 276.2 per cent of exports ten years later. Foreign debt also rose from $1.2 billion in

1980 to $5.1 billion a decade later. Inflation soared, with an increase of 980 per cent during the 1980s. All these statistics translated into the reality of a sharp decline in the standard of living, with progressively higher prices for imported goods as Afghan currency fell in value, in turn causing families to struggle against impossible odds to feed themselves and their children amidst all the other consequences of the war.

Why the Mujahideen won

The Mujahideen suffered from a number of weaknesses, some significant enough to have compromised success had not the defects of their opponents loomed so much larger. Riven with factionalism and never remotely able to coalesce in order to provide a single, unified form of military opposition either to DRA or Soviet forces, the Mujahideen comprised more than 30 groups seeking a wide array of differing political, social, economic, and religious objectives – hence the dreadful internecine struggle which emerged after the fall of Najibullah's regime in 1992. No single government-in-exile represented the political interests of the rebel movement as a whole, and while a council representing the main factions did exist in Pakistan with agreement between them to rotate the senior leading role every three months, in the course of the war at least some of the various factions nevertheless fought each other intermittently, as well as the DRA and Soviets continuously. Such factionalism might have undone the whole thread of resistance; and yet, paradoxically, these very divisions also served as a source of strength, since the Soviets and DRA encountered serious problems striking at such fragmented entities, whether their leadership cadres, specifically, or their armed forces, generally.

However generous the level of aid provided to the various groups by the United States and many other donors, the Mujahideen as a whole could not agree on the division of such largesse, some of which filtered through Pakistan, some via Iran – Sunni and Shi'a

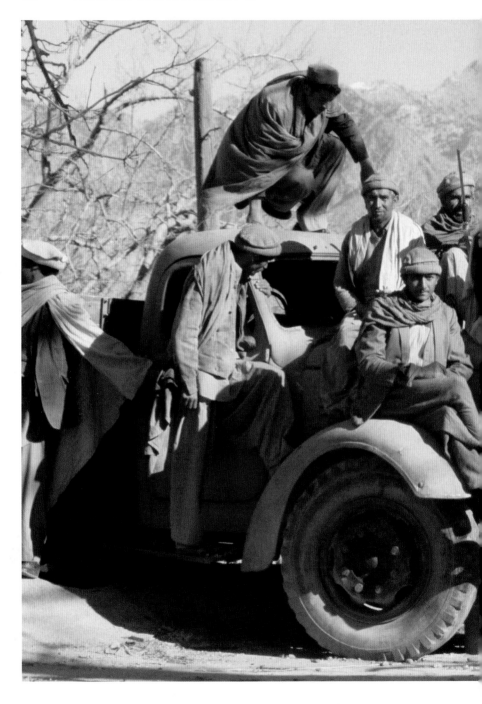

By their nature, the Mujahideen preferred noisy, direct attacks that brought them into close contact with their opponents, as opposed to acts of sabotage. (Photo by Pascal Manoukian/ Sygma via Getty Images)

majority countries, respectively – and therefore each with different political and ideological agendas in Afghanistan. External funding consequently became unevenly distributed and much was lost through theft and corruption. Nevertheless, external aid played a critical role in Mujahideen success. US assistance alone exceeded $2 billion in total from 1980 to 1988, inclusive, and non-lethal American aid is thought to have approximately matched that amount. As an entirely separate funding stream, military aid provided covertly by the CIA exceeded $650 million in 1987 alone.

Such vast sums assumed tangible form. While the insurgents began their fight against the Soviets with light arms, by the end of 1988 their arsenals boasted a range of sophisticated weapons furnished by a range of international donors, supplemented by captured arms, including armour, APCs, light artillery, and howitzers, albeit in small numbers. To this, in far greater quantity, the resistance could boast multiple rocket launchers, several types of Western-made light surface-to-air missile systems, mortars, shoulder- and tripod-mounted rocket launchers, recoilless rifles, anti-aircraft guns of various calibres, and of course the ubiquitous grenade launchers. Not only did the Mujahideen gradually acquire more advanced weapons – such as the man-portable surface-to-air missiles which mitigated, as previously noted, the helicopter threat – but they adapted to changing circumstances over time better than their rivals, making improved use of a range of weapons, especially artillery, small arms, and mines.

While they failed to capture a city or deprive the Soviets of any of their major military installations or camps, knowingly or not the resistance embraced Clausewitz's dictum that such objectives do not constitute the enemy's centre of gravity. Anticipating the 21st century epigram associated with the West's war against the Taliban, 'You have the watches, but we have the time', the Mujahideen remained undaunted in the face of their enemy's superior technology and firepower, and applied sufficient pressure over a protracted period so as to exact a price in human and material terms which ultimately exceeded the Kremlin's ability to pay. In short, the guerrillas understood that notwithstanding defeat in nearly every tactical action, continuing the fight would ultimately reap dividends at the strategic level.

Final words

The Soviet–Afghan War demonstrated that the Soviets had embarked on an adventure based on unattainable goals. They sought to uphold a manifestly weak and unpopular government and in so doing, especially after violating Afghan soil, shattered any degree of legitimacy that the regime might have hoped to garner from the Afghan people. When Taraki's communist regime came to power in Kabul in 1978 it failed to recognize that the bulk of Afghan society, based as it was on tribal structures with nothing in common with Marxist ideology, did not desire fundamental change to its way of life, not least reforms foisted upon it from outside that represented a direct threat to centuries of tradition and religious conviction. Thus, when the Kabul regime and its PDPA apparatus, activists, functionaries, and KhAD agents spread across the country with revolutionary fervour, they unwittingly propelled Afghanistan into civil war, with Soviet intervention to prop up the regime exponentially worsening the existing domestic strife to appalling levels of misery and physical devastation, splitting the country along even deeper factional lines than before and encouraging Islamic extremism to boot.

The war also revealed, as had Vietnam for the Americans 20 years earlier, that victory remains elusive even for a superpower when it confronts an opponent driven by deep ideological or religious convictions and bolstered morally, but above all materially, by generous external allies. Like the Vietminh and Viet Cong in the 1950s and '60s, the Mujahideen proved themselves an exceedingly formidable force with which to reckon, notwithstanding their initial acute deficiencies in weapons, ammunition, and supplies. Once adequately armed, equipped, and fed, and with access to safe havens providing training and rest, the motivation and drive of an exceptionally robust, utterly determined, ideologically driven foe employing tactics suited to the circumstances produced the most intractable of opponents: with time on their side and a willingness to accept horrific losses many times in excess of their adversaries. Herein lay the ingredients of the Soviet Union's military demise and the concomitant ruins of its political ambitions in the region.

The Soviets' failure derived partly from the political hubris of politicians, who grievously underestimated the colossal scale of the enterprise on which they embarked in 1979. (REUTERS/ Sergei Karpukhin)

CHRONOLOGY

1965	**1 January** People's Democratic Party of Afghanistan (PDPA) is founded, giving the communists a stake in Afghan politics.
1973	**July** Mohammad Daoud Khan (1909–78) ends the 40-year reign of King Mohammad Zahir Shah (1915–2007) in a palace coup.
1978	**17 April** President Daoud is assassinated in a communist coup led by Nur Mohammad Taraki, who appoints himself head of state and begins a reign of terror against political opponents.
1979	**15–21 March** Anti-communist demonstrators seize control of Herat; the Afghan 15th Division, ordered to retake the city, deserts to the resistance. Afghan and Soviet air forces bomb the city, killing an estimated 5,000 civilians.

17 March Soviet Politburo debates question of internal situation in Afghanistan.

20 March Despite Taraki's urgent request for Soviet intervention in the Afghan civil war, Soviet Foreign Minister Aleksei Kosygin (1904–80) declines, fearing escalation of violence.

April Helicopters manned by Soviet pilots in support of a DRA offensive in the Kunar Valley destroy the village of Kerala, killing approximately 1,000 people.

17 May Mechanized brigade of the Afghan 7th Division defects to the Mujahideen in Paktia province.

August 5th Brigade of the Afghan 9th Division mutinies and supports the rebels in the Kunar Valley.

14 September Troops loyal to Prime Minister Hafizullah Amin kill Taraki, facilitating Amin's accession to power.

4 November Iranian militants storm the US

Embassy in Tehran, inadvertently diverting the attention of the Carter administration from deteriorating events in Afghanistan.

12 December Soviet Politburo reaches decision for invasion of Afghanistan.

24 December Soviet air assault forces arrive in Kabul by air.

27 December Large-scale Soviet forces cross into Afghanistan by road and proceed south; Soviet air assault and Spetsnaz forces stage a coup in Kabul and kill Amin.

28 December Babrak Karmal (1929–96) appointed new head of state of the Democratic Republic of Afghanistan.

1980

1 January Revolt in Kandahar results in deaths of Soviet troops and citizens by mob violence.

January United Nations condemns the Soviet invasion.

February Soviet forces conduct sweep of Kunar Valley.

21 February Soviet troops and KGB forces kill hundreds and arrest thousands (many later executed) of Afghans protesting the occupation of their country; massive demonstrations in Kabul; anti-Soviet riot suppressed by Soviet forces in Shindand, in Farah province.

March Soviet offensive in Paktia province; second sweep of Kunar Valley.

April Soviet offensive in Panjshir Valley.

May Soviet forces sweep Ghazni province; third sweep of Kunar Valley.

June Second sweep of Ghazni province.

September Fourth sweep of Kunar Valley; *Panjshir I* offensive.

October *Panjshir II* offensive.

November Fifth sweep of Kunar Valley; sweep of Wardak province; Soviet offensive in Lowghar Valley until mid-December.

1981

20 January Ronald Reagan (1911–2004) succeeds Jimmy Carter (1924–) as US president.

February–March Fighting in Kandahar.
April *Panjshir III* offensive.
June–July Soviet offensive in Nangarhar province.
4 July Offensive in Sarobi Valley in Paktika province; fighting in Herat.
August *Panjshir IV* offensive.
5 September Offensive in Farah province.
October Soviet sweep around Herat; offensive in Kandahar.
December Sweep in Nangarhar province; fighting in Herat.

1982   **January** Fighting in Herat.
1 January Javier Pérez de Cuéllar (1920–2020) succeeds Kurt Waldheim (1918–2007) as UN Secretary General.
February Urban fighting in Kandahar.
May *Panjshir V* offensive, launched in retaliation for Mujahideen attack on Bagram air base.
July Sweep of Paghman Hills west of Kabul.
August–September *Panjshir VI* offensive.
November Offensive in Laghman Valley.
10 November Brezhnev dies; succeeded by Yuri Andropov (1914–84) as General Secretary of the Communist Party of the Soviet Union.

1983   **January** Offensive in Lowghar Valley.
February UN Secretary General discusses Soviet withdrawal with Andropov.
April Sweep around Herat.
June Offensive in Ghazni province.
August Offensive in Paktia province.
November Offensive in Shomali Valley.

1984   **9 February** Andropov dies; succeeded by Konstantin Chernenko (1911–85) as General Secretary of the Communist Party of the Soviet Union.
April *Panjshir VII* offensive.
June Offensive in the Lowghar Valley; offensives around Herat and Kandahar.
July–August Offensive in Lowghar and Shomali valleys.
August–October Soviet forces relieve garrison of Ali

Kheyl in Paktia province.

September *Panjshir VIII* offensive.

October Fighting in Herat.

November Operation in Paktia province.

December Offensive in Kunar Valley.

1985   **10 March** Chernenko dies; succeeded by Mikhail Gorbachev.

April Offensive in the Maidan Valley in Wardak province.

May–June Offensive in Kunar province and relief of the garrison at Barikowt.

June *Panjshir IX* offensive.

July Fighting in Herat and Kandahar.

August–September Offensive in Paktia province; Khost is relieved but Soviet forces fail to capture Zhawar.

October Soviet Politburo decides troops should leave Afghanistan within 18 months.

1986   **February** Gorbachev announces to 27th Soviet Party Congress that troops will leave Afghanistan.

March Offensive around Andkhvoy.

April Zhawar captured during offensive in Paktia province.

May Offensive near Kandahar.

5 May Mohammad Najibullah (1947–96) replaces Karmal as People's Democratic Party of Afghanistan (PDPA) General Secretary and effective head of state.

c. **June–August** Soviets withdraw 15,000 troops from Afghanistan.

June Offensive in Khejob Valley.

August Offensive in Lowghar Valley.

September First Stinger missiles deployed in action by Mujahideen, bringing down three helicopters.

October Withdrawal of six Soviet regiments.

November Offensive in Mizan Valley in Oruzgan province.

1987   **May–June** Offensive in Paktia province.

November Start of Soviets' Operation *Magistral* to relieve Khost.

December Khost relieved; Gorbachev and Reagan discuss Afghanistan at the Washington Summit.

1988   **March** Offensive in Paktika province to relieve Orgun.

April Offensive between Kandahar and Ghazni.

14 April Conclusion of Geneva Accords, which had begun informally three years before; agreements for Soviet withdrawal.

May–August Large-scale withdrawals by 40th Army from various points in Afghanistan.

15 October Strength of Soviet forces in Afghanistan down by half to approximately 60,000.

November Start of second phase of large-scale withdrawals by 40th Army from various points in Afghanistan, but mainly the south.

1989   **20 January** George H. W. Bush (1924–2018) succeeds Ronald Reagan as US president.

15 February Withdrawal of the last Soviet combat units from Afghanistan.

1992   **15–16 April** Najibullah's regime collapses.

August Russian Embassy in Kabul evacuated.

1996   **September** Taliban forces capture Kabul and execute Najibullah.

2001   **11 September** al-Qaeda launches terrorist attacks against the United States, killing 3,000 people in the Twin Towers in New York and others at the Pentagon in Washington and aboard an airliner which crashes in the Pennsylvania countryside.

December US and UK forces, together with those of the Afghan Northern Alliance, oust the Taliban from government; thereafter, other NATO forces arrive to oppose continued Taliban resistance and to drive al-Qaeda from the country.

FURTHER READING

Alexiev, Alex, *Inside the Soviet Army in Afghanistan* (Rand Corporation, 1988)

Alexievich, Svetlana, *Boys in Zinc* (Penguin Classics, 2017)

Anderson, Jon Lee, *Guerrilla: Journeys in the Insurgent World* (Abacus, 2006)

Arnold, Anthony, *Afghanistan: The Soviet Invasion in Perspective* (Hoover Institution Press, 1985)

Arnold, Anthony, *The Fateful Pebble: Afghanistan's Role in the Fall of the Soviet Empire* (Presidio Press, 1993)

Aspaturian, Dallin, et al., *The Soviet Invasion of Afghanistan: Three Perspectives* (University of California Press, 1996)

Barfield, Thomas, *Afghanistan: A Cultural and Political History* (Princeton UP, 2012)

Bocharov, Gennady, *Russian Roulette: Afghanistan through Russian Eyes* (HarperCollins, 1990)

Bonner, Arthur, *Among the Afghans* (Duke UP, 1987)

Borer, Douglas, *Superpowers Defeated: Vietnam and Afghanistan Compared* (Routledge, 1999)

Borovik, Artyom, *The Hidden War: A Russian Journalist's Account of the Soviet War in Afghanistan* (Grove Press, 2001)

Bradsher, Henry, *Afghanistan and the Soviet Union* (Duke UP, 1983)

Bradsher, Henry, *Afghan Communism and Soviet Intervention* (OUP, 1999)

Braithwaite, Rodric, *Afgantsy: The Russians in Afghanistan, 1979–89* (Profile Books, 2011)

Brigot, André, and Roy, Olivier, *The War in Afghanistan* (Harvester Wheatsheaf, 1988)

Campbell, David, *Soviet Paratrooper vs Mujahideen Fighter* (Osprey, 2017)

Collins, Joseph, *The Soviet Invasion of Afghanistan: A Study in the Use of Force* (D.C. Heath Canada, 1986)

Collins, Kathleen, *The Logic of Clan Politics in Central Asia* (CUP, 2006)

Cordesman, Anthony and Wagner, Abraham, *The Lessons of Modern War. Vol. III: The Afghan and Falklands Conflicts* (Westview Press, 1990)

Cordovez, Diego and Harrison, Selig, *Out of Afghanistan: The Inside Story of the Soviet Withdrawal* (OUP, 1995)

Crile, George, *Charlie Wilson's War: The Extraordinary Account of the Largest Covert Operation in History* (Atlantic Monthly Press, 2003)

Dimitrakis, Panagiotis, *The Secret War in Afghanistan: The Soviet Union, China, and Anglo-American Intelligence in the Afghan War* (I.B. Tauris, 2013)

Dupree, Louis, *Afghanistan* (OUP, 1997)

Emadi, Hafizullah, *Culture and Customs of Afghanistan* (Greenwood, 2005)

Ewans, Martin, *Afghanistan: A Short History of Its People and Politics* (HarperCollins, 2002)

Feifer, Gregory, *The Great Gamble: The Soviet War in Afghanistan* (HarperPerennial, 2010)

Fenzel, Michael, *No Miracles: The Failure of Decision-Making in the Afghan War* (Stanford Security Studies, 2017)

Fremont-Barnes, Gregory, *The Anglo-Afghan Wars 1839–1919* (Osprey, 2009)

Galeotti, Mark, *Afghanistan: The Soviet Union's Last War* (Routledge, 2001)

Galeotti, Mark, *The Panjshir Valley, 1980–1986: The Lion Tames the Bear in Afghanistan* (Osprey, 2021)

Gall, Sandy, *Afghanistan: Agony of a Nation* (Bodley Head, 1988)

Gall, Sandy, *Afghanistan: Travels with the Mujahedeen* (New English Library, 1989)

Gandomi, J., *Lessons from the Soviet Occupation in Afghanistan for the United States and NATO* (Princeton UP, 2008)

Girardet, Edward, *Afghanistan: The Soviet War* (New York, NY: St. Martin's Press, 1985)

Giustozzi, Antonio, *War, Politics and Society in Afghanistan, 1978–1992* (Hurst & Co., 2000)

Goodson, Larry, *Afghanistan's Endless War: State Failure, Regional Politics, and the Rise of the Taliban* (University of Washington Press, 2001)

Grasselli, Gabriella, *British and American Responses to the Soviet Invasion of Afghanistan* (Dartmouth Publishing, 1996)

Grau, Lester, *The Bear Went Over the Mountain: Soviet Combat Tactics in Afghanistan* (Routledge, 1988)

Grau, Lester, and Gress, Michael, *The Soviet–Afghan War: How a Superpower Fought and Lost* (University Press of Kansas, 2002)

Hammond, T., *Red Flag over Afghanistan: The Communist Coup, the Soviet Invasion and the Consequences* (Westview Press, 1984)

Hauner, Milan, *The Soviet War in Afghanistan: Patterns of Russian Imperialism* (University Press of America, 1991)

Hyman, Anthony, *Afghanistan under Soviet Domination, 1964–91* (Macmillan, 1992)

Isby, David, *Russia's War in Afghanistan* (Osprey, 1986)

Isby, David, *War in a Distant Country: Afghanistan – Invasion and Resistance* (Arms and Armour Press, 1989)

Jalali, Ali Ahmad, and Grau, Lester, *Afghan Guerrilla Warfare: In the Words of the Mujahideen Fighters* (Compendium Publishing, 2001)

Jalali, Ali Ahmad, and Grau, Lester, *The Other Side of the Mountain: Mujahideen Tactics in the Soviet–Afghan War* (Military Press, 2001)

Johnson, Rob, *The Afghan Way of War – Culture and Pragmatism: A Critical History* (Hurst & Co., 2011)

Jones, Ellen, *Red Army and Society: A Sociology of the Soviet Military* (Allen & Unwin, 1985)

Kakar, Hasan, *Afghanistan: The Soviet Invasion and the Afghan Response, 1979–82* (University of California Press, 1997)

Kaplan, Robert, *Soldiers of God: With Islamic Warriors in Afghanistan and Pakistan* (Vintage Books, 2001)

Keller, Shoshana, *To Moscow, Not Mecca: The Soviet Campaign against Islam in Central Asia* (Praeger Publishing, 2001)

Khan, Riaz, *Untying the Knot: Negotiating Soviet Withdrawal* (Duke UP, 1991)

Loyn, David, *Butcher and Bolt* (Windmill Books, 2009)

McMichael, Scott, *Stumbling Bear: Soviet Military Performance in Afghanistan* (Brassey's, 1991)

Magnus, Ralph, and Naby, Eden, *Afghanistan: Mullah, Marx and Mujahid* (West View Press, 1998)

Maley, William, *The Afghanistan Wars* (Palgrave Macmillan, 2009)

Mendelson, Sarah, *Changing Course: Ideas, Politics, and the Soviet Withdrawal from Afghanistan* (Princeton UP, 1998)

Ministry of Defence, United Kingdom, *Army Field Manual. Vol. 1, Part 10: Countering Insurgency* (MoD, 2010)

Nojumi, Neamatollah, *The Rise of the Taliban in Afghanistan* (Palgrave Macmillan, 2002)

Odom, W., *The Collapse of the Soviet Military* (Yale UP, 1998)

Prado, J., *Safe for Democracy: The Secret Wars of the CIA* (Ivar R. Dee, 2006)

Rasanaygam, Angelo, *Afghanistan: A Modern History* (I.B. Tauris, 2005)

Ro'i, Yaacov, *The Bleeding Wound: The Soviet War in Afghanistan and the Collapse of the Soviet System* (Stanford University Press, 2022)

Roy, Olivier, *Islam and Resistance in Afghanistan* (CUP, 1986)

Roy, Olivier, *The Lessons of the Soviet–Afghan War* (Nuffield Press, 1991)

Rubin, Barnett, *The Fragmentation of Afghanistan* (Yale UP, 1995)

Russian General Staff, ed. Lester Grau and Michael Gress, *The Soviet–Afghan War: How a Superpower Fought and Lost* (University Press of Kansas, 2002)

Saikal, Amin, *Modern Afghanistan: A History of Struggle and Survival* (I.B. Tauris, 2004)

Saikal, Amin, and Maley, William, *The Soviet Withdrawal from Afghanistan* (CUP, 1989)

Sarin, Oleg, and Dvoretsky, Lev, *The Afghan Syndrome: The Soviet Union's Vietnam* (Presidio Press, 1993)

Schein, Zammis, *Soviet and Mujahideen Uniforms, Clothing, and Equipment in the Soviet-Afghan War, 1979–1989* (Schiffer Publishing, 2016)

Schofield, Carey, *The Russian Elite: Inside Spetsnaz and the Airborne Forces* (Greenhill Books, 1993)

Tamarov, Vladislav, *Afghanistan: A Russian Soldier's Story* (Ten Speed Press, 2005)

Tanner, S., *Afghanistan: A Military History from Alexander the Great to the War Against the Taliban* (Perseus Books Group, 2009)

Tomsen, Peter, *The Wars of Afghanistan: Messianic Terrorism, Tribal Conflicts, and the Failure of Great Powers* (Public Affairs, 2011)

Urban, Mark, *War in Afghanistan* (Macmillan, 1990)

Weinbaum, Martin, *Pakistan and Afghanistan: Resistance and Reconstruction* (Westview Press, 1994)

Yousaf, Mohammad, and Adkin, Mark, *The Battle for Afghanistan: The Soviets Versus the Mujahideen during the 1980s* (Pen & Sword, 2007)

INDEX